My Memoir of Love, Loss, Deception, and Finding Myself Through It All

Nina Samuel

ISBN 979-8-89409-371-0

Dedication

To my dearest grandchildren, with love, I share this piece of my heart, a story filled with the experiences that made me who I am today.

Acknowledgements

A special shout-out to the nameless individuals whose existence I won't directly glorify by mentioning names (you know who you are), a heartfelt "thank you." Your brand of chaos, though unwelcome at the time, served as the finest creative lighter fluid. You fueled a fire I didn't even know existed, a burning need to tell my story. Consider this a public thank-you note disguised as a petty swipe. While you may have intended to knock me down, you inadvertently launched me towards this book. So, in a begrudging way, thanks for the assist.

Now, for the rest of you wonderful souls who deserve recognition, thanks for becoming my light source.

This rollercoaster wouldn't have made it to the station if I didn't have you in my life.

About the Author

Nina Samuel is a courageous writer who once resided on a small, peaceful island, but life seemed to have different plans for her. Her transformation from a small-town girl to a big city was where her story began. Her journey was shaped by the sharp contrast between her island home's innocence and city life's guarded reality.

Leaving a place where trust was as familiar as the scent of salt air for a more concrete place where suspicion lingers in the shadows was a culture shock unlike any other. The warmth of open doors and friendly smiles was replaced by a constant need for vigilance.

In the big city, the very people she trusted most often became the ones who taught her the harshest lessons. Jealousy and envy, which were alienated concepts to her, were now her reality. But while a strong exterior became her shield, it couldn't fully mask the vulnerability beneath.

Throughout her journey, she felt as if there was no room for her weakness to find solace. But as a mother of two, she was not allowed to submerge herself in the darkness—at least for the sake of her children. Whenever her children needed a lighthouse, she became the vigil.

With the scars of abandonment that she faced and the betrayals that hardened her, she aimed to become stronger every passing day while spreading courage among others.

Within these pages, you'll discover the woman behind the mask—a woman fiercely protective, with a heart scarred but not broken.

Preface

This autobiography is an unflinching look at my life—a woman who was punished into the fires of betrayal and misunderstanding.

At this crossroad of my life, when I turn the pages of my past, I find myself drawn back to the wide-eyed innocence of my youth. Growing up, I was like any other child, full of dreams and aspirations, with a heart full of hope and a mind full of curiosity. But soon, my illusion about life was shattered. Once, a child with nothing to offer but love was now covered with scars.

The most trusted ones betrayed me—not once but multiple times, and the bruises embossed on my heart still scream for my truth; I was left at the mercy of this world. I made mistakes, and I had to learn to stand by them. I was misunderstood and struggled to find my place in the world. Look at the cruelty of people; they tried to push me down the cliff when I stood on the edge. Nobody held onto me; nobody saved me or wanted to save me.

But despite it all, I refused to fall into the trap of evil. I held on to the courage and learned to rise above the pain. And as I look back on my journey so far, I am proud of the person I have become. I am proud of the strength I have found, the wisdom I have gained, and the love I have shared.

This book is not a mere story but a chronicle holding my trial. It is a record of how I learned to live my life despite the obstacles that stood in my way. And I hope that by sharing my journey, I can inspire others to do the same. They need to find the strength to rise above their own struggles, learn from their mistakes, and never give up on their dreams.

Contents

Chapter 1

"See, I think there are roads that lead us to each other. But in my family, there were no roads - just underground tunnels. I think we all got lost in those underground tunnels. No, not lost. We just lived there."

- Benjamin Alire Sáenz

Today, when I sit down to share the story of my childhood, I find it hard to believe all the disruptive and chaotic days that I have stood up to from my age of naivety have become a part of my past. How can I ever forget the journey where I learned the ugly truth of life?

My story begins in the southern part of Trinidad and Tobago, where my destiny pushed me to live my life far away in the coziness of Victoria County. It was a place I've called home for as long as I can remember. It wasn't a village, nor was it a metropolitan city with honking and pollution; instead, it was a small town where everyone knew everyone and your neighbors were as close as family. We lived in houses so close together that it felt like one big extended family whose doors were always wide open, and windows revealed a community full of warmth and inviting energy.

I was born into this close-knit world, where my grandparent's house was the initial backdrop for my early years. To tell you the truth, my grandfather lived in a grand house with spacious rooms and church floors, and it was because of his beautiful house the light of the home my parents built was dimmed. This new home that my parents made was of a wooden structure raised on stilts.

Living there felt different after we spent time with my grandparents at his high-end shelter. Even in the eyes of society, our house was considered a "poor house"; it was below the sub-standard. We had dirt floors, and electricity had yet to make its way into our lives. But to me, it was simply home. Even though the lack of electricity instilled the fear of darkness in me, I would have been the happiest to call it my home if my parents were a little more concerned about our happiness.

Sometimes, when I stole glimpses of other people's houses, I started feeling discontent with my living standards. As I entered a different phase of life, I became increasingly aware of the differences between the large, American dream-style houses I saw on television and my small, timber dwelling. Sitting alone, I often daydreamed while wondering about luxurious homes, splendid surroundings, and a life filled with better things. I yearned to have my own place where I could retreat at any time and call my own. But my reality was far different from my imagination. I was sharing a bed and a room with my siblings.

In many ways, I felt my life was a piece of work. My father used to disappear for days, only to reappear in a cloud of dust and diesel exhaust while his heavy-duty trucks rumbled into our driveway. Even though he was primarily absent, my childhood perception of him was that of a good man, a loving father at heart. However, beneath that kind of exterior lay a fierce storm that was not a mysterious tale for us. The grim reality was that my dad's childhood had been tarnished by abuse. He was a target of his stepmother's wrath, and so, growing up in a household that offered him nothing but visible scars, he struggled to contain his anger, often letting it spill over for the slightest reasons. If I had to compare his anger to anything, I would say it was a hurricane with no apparent warning, and we, his children, were unwittingly caught in its destructive path.

My father's weekend ritual involved drinking alcohol, which was particularly deceitful, often ending up in screaming and fighting. Even though ages and ages have passed and now I have turned into an adult, the tormented child that once confined itself within me still remembers every minute detail of the dreadful scene – my parents' loud, horrifying fights, the screeching voices, they instilled a sense of impending doom in every passerby. As members of that household, all we could do was resort to complete silence, look for a safe corner of our house, and make sure that we stayed out of my father's sight before he harmed any of us.

As a kid, I always felt it was normal, day-to-day bickering in every neighborhood. But for some reason, my heart never accepted this grim reality. Perhaps my subconsciousness was able to see through the eerie atmosphere we were forced to live in, so we started looking for ways to escape the pandemonium that our father carefully carved for us. But, deep inside, I always yearned to find a place that could smell like home – a place that would take me in its embrace against the harshness of the outer world. So, in turn, my siblings and I found an escape route to our aunt's house to avoid the chaos that would unfold at home at any given hour of the day. But we never realized that no matter how beautiful the escape was, at the end of the day, we had to return to this imprisonment.

Even though so many years have passed, I can still feel the terror, the shaking, and the intense panic that choked me during those times. My hands tremble as I write about the day I encountered the intensity of my father's anger that struck us like an unpredictable storm. I became cautious, tiptoeing around him, fearing that the slightest misstep would ignite his rage.

There were instances when my father not only directed his anger at my mother but turned his wrath towards us, his own flesh and blood. I vividly remember a time when he tried to throw a table at my baby sister because she refused to go to him. But, you see, she was just a baby who was unfortunately born into a family that was led by a man bound to misogynistic tendencies. I have always said that our fates were damned because we were born in a family where women were asked to cover the crimes of men. It was a woman's responsibility to domesticate the man and turn him into a human, but on the other hand, men were free to live their lives as if they were born to be wild.

However, what makes my heart bleed is the fact that my father was not always this vile. His anger was always fueled when he was under the influence or intoxicated. But, when he was sober, a different man emerged within him. Surprisingly, he was never bothered by my mother's occupation. He did not mind her working as well. When clear-headed, my father was extremely patient with us. Despite my abhor toward his anger management issues, I believe it to be my duty to tell people that he was a loving, doting father who adored his children, not to mention when sober. However, the memories of his wrath overshadowed all these moments of happiness and love.

As I have said earlier, my father had his own story. There was a time when he was a pure, young child looking for answers to his miserable faith. On different occasions, his family members had shared stories of his traumatic childhood, where he was abused by his stepmother, enduring physical and emotional torment that scarred him for life.

The traces of his shattered self that I discovered as his daughter made me change my perception of him from a man who cannot control his anger issues to a survivor of a horrific childhood. This was not the justification for his actions, but I felt empathy for the pain he endured. Again, it didn't excuse his behavior, but as his daughter, I realized he was not always callous. At least I knew that his past had left him wounded, unable to cope with his anger. He was a man reaching out for help and wasn't evil, but the world let him down.

No one attempted to connect with him when he sought someone to depend on, prompting him to internalize all his anger. Eventually, he resurrected this pent-up fury. I reckon it led him to reflect his trauma and anxiety onto us, subjecting us to a comparable, if not greater, level of anguish. This encapsulates the irony of my existence - daily, I endured the legacy of generational trauma, yet I adamantly declined to perpetuate it to future generations. I transformed into a resilient foundation because I felt accountable for shielding them from witnessing the world's darker facets.

My parents' relationship was far from perfect. I never witnessed them sharing a loving moment, a meal, or even sitting together peacefully. Their interactions were always about arguments and strife, leaving me to wonder why they couldn't find happiness together. Why were they not like other couples? Their constant battle made me lose hope in myself – what if this misery never ended? But after all, someone had to end this destruction, so at an age when I should be playing outside with other children, I decided to use my parents' relationship as the guide for what I didn't want in my future relationships.

Perhaps that is why I always believed that I was a gifted child or, precisely, a special child with a clear vision of right or wrong. In my head, I was the main character who could achieve almost everything and anything. I don't remember who fed on my delusion, but for me, my vision and the imaginary scenarios I created were absolute decrees, and in any case, I took them seriously. All the same, I was sure of my power, but discerning life's verity was not child's play yet; here I was, characterizing right from wrong while defining who the real God was. It was a responsibility that was bestowed over me not by God himself but by my parents, who married outside their religion. My father was a Christian, while my mother followed the Hindu religion. During those days, marrying outside of faith was not a well-received idea, and people usually detested children born from such marriages. Even though I had yet to experience such bitter incidents, I knew one thing for a fact: I could not live the rest of my life as an outsider alienated by society. It was also a ritual in my family where my parents coerced me into attending Sunday school early in the morning at 7. Ironically, they were the ones who never accompanied us to the classes.

My mother, who wanted me to follow her religion, also tried to mold my mind toward Hinduism, intending to make me feel more inclined toward this particular religion, but deep inside, I was sure of my faith. I knew what I had to do and which route to take to reach my destination – the road that could lead me to the ultimate truth: Christianity. So, once again, at a tender age, I stood up for myself and decided never to lose the string connecting me to God.

Readers, you may find it odd that a child so young could be gifted with the power of divinity, and in all honesty, I believe defining my relationship with God as something transcendental could be an overstatement. Nonetheless, my love and adoration for my religion persisted until the end. But it did create an invisible boundary between my mother and me. Yet, she continued introducing me to her religion, hoping that I could follow polytheism, but not even for a split second I felt inclined towards any other religion but Christianity. My faith was about devoting oneself to the Almighty, so I did.

Nevertheless, I respected my mother's religion and hoped she would have appreciated my preferences, too. I recall an early memory of when my mother forced me to attend her religious activities. I cried and protested, but it was as if my mother could not hear me. She paid no heed to my fear and left me traumatized for my life. The reason behind my extreme reaction to my mother's religion was not because I never decided to understand her; instead, it was because of my early exposure to myths that made me close my heart to polytheism. Besides that, it was a known fact in my family that some demons or evil spirits possessed my mother, and I, being minor, did not waste another minute to come up with the presumption that these were the consequences of following prey to polytheism.

Certainly, I was too young to understand the intricacy of the relationship between religions, and as much as my ignorance is to be blamed here, I was never educated on the beauty of different religions. Even though I had friends who were Hindu, my mother never bothered sharing the insight of her religion; instead, for her, dumping Hinduism over us was the easy way out. Maybe, just maybe, if she had the patience to teach us about her religion, her children would have learned to better understand other religions. But then again, my mother disregarded our fears because taming us might have been better than educating us. You see, her one wrong decision, and I feared the nexus of mortals and immortals. I remember asking my grandfather what if he returned as a spirit after his soul departed. My grandfather, who was my world and the only person who ever made me feel loved, looked at me with his Duchenne smile and said, *"I will return as a butterfly."* The pure, playful conversation ended in no time with my grandfather and I distracted in our little zone.

After a little while, my grandfather ended up leaving this world. I remember those days when we briefly stayed at my grandfather's house before he moved to his last yet permanent abode. That was the first time when I experienced the excruciating pain that comes with death. I was too young to let my mind understand the concept of death; even then, my heart was bleeding from the inside, and I could feel what it was like to be genuinely melancholic. I could feel the wretchedness of my heart because the only person who gave meaning to my existence left me stranded at a junction where I could rely on no one.

Chapter 2

"A young outcast will often feel that there is something wrong with himself, but as he gets older, grows more confident in who he is, he will adapt, he will begin to feel that there is something wrong with everyone else."

- Criss Jami

I have always been a child who lived in her fantasy world where my thoughts wandered in a land free from all the aches and sufferings. I believed all my pains and miseries could be ended if I chose to move to a different place—I thought it was the city that was holding me back from attaining what I desired the most. As if my destiny took my fury a little seriously this time, it started carving the route in my life for its most significant plot twist. It all started when I left my homeland behind to move to New York City—a city that never sleeps. I clearly remember the sensation that weaved into my skin when the plane touched down at JFK. It was a cold December day when the chills of the city took over my consciousness, making me reconsider the image of New York that I had envisioned in my dreams to this date.

The city held the picture of towering buildings, and here I was in the middle, wondering whether I could ever become a part of them. But honestly, the image was not the awe-inspiring skyline for me. Perhaps because I was jet-lagged, the eerie vibes in the breezy atmosphere set a cold and somewhat gloomy overtone. From the moment we landed on this foreign ground, I felt discomfort that constantly reminded me that real life can never be the same as reel life. My mother, who came to pick us up at the airport, could identify our longing for the lives we had left behind, so she took us to McDonald's as a gesture to welcome us for the first time. In the middle of consuming what was my first meal of the day, I realized how different my life used to be. Back in my home country, eating out at an outlet like this was a rare sight; here, it was a daily ritual for the citizens of this crowded city. But, the excitement of being in America soon gave way to homesickness, and my day ended with a realization that this was my reality and not a show airing on national television from now on; my siblings and I had to bid goodbye to our previous simple lifestyle while settling into a city that we had yet to discover.

While perfectly concealing my excitement, we visited the American school system and enrolled directly into the 12th grade based on my academic performance. The school was in the borough of Queens, where I was stuck in a sea of diversity with not-so-familiar accents and varied fashion styles. However, this fancy place soon removed its veil and portrayed its ugly truth – the reality that the lives of bourgeois people never mattered to the elite world. People like us amounted to nothing in their eyes.

Given my financial status, I was made to feel like an outsider by the people who were the same age as me but had lived in their own bubble of reality. They were so privileged that they never had to grasp the reality of people like us struggling to make ends meet. Even though I have lived a pretty tough life myself, on that day, I battled with the embarrassment of not fitting in, followed by the fact that I lacked high-end brands and trendy clothes. As a teenager who was already fighting to find her identity in society,

I wondered what if I had the same lifestyle as them— maybe I would have fit in well among them.

But now, when I think about those days, I see them as a phase—a passing cloud that will progress sooner or later. During those days, attending mere classes used to flood my head with worries, and every trivial matter intimidated me. I remember a whole lot about the school that overwhelmed me. Everything was a dreading process, from the enormous school building to the routine security measures. For a person like me, who came from a simple town, metal detectors and security checks in school were not usual to witness. All these sudden changes imposed on my life made me feel like an alien deported to a foreign planet who was now struggling to adapt to a world that seemed light-years away from what I had known.

Nonetheless, I had moved to a new location, leaving behind my old life, and now I had to try to make an effort to assimilate before I became an outcast, but through what means? We were barely surviving in New York with almost no money at our disposal. So, I started working tirelessly, securing a job at 15 and earning a mere $100 a week. However, the amount I made was insufficient to fulfill my dream since I faced the daunting task of contributing to my family's bills. My job required me to be separated from my family while residing with an unknown family in exchange for caring for the landlord's child and performing household chores. No matter how much chaos my family was, staying with complete strangers tore me apart, but I had no other choice. I had to earn for the sake of my family—I had to abandon my dreams to fulfill theirs, and so I gave in to slavery.

Every Friday, with a heart filled with joy, I returned to the tiny basement apartment I shared with my siblings. But the unfortunate part was that the moment I stepped into that house, my hard-earned $100 used to disappear into the household expenses. Every month, I used to decide on the budget to purchase some clothes, but my mother always took every penny of mine and left me with nothing for myself. I never understood why I had worked so tirelessly when my money had to vanish in thin air. And would they have accepted me if I was never making this much money? All these questions were instilled in me by the mere desire to belong and be loved.

I yearned to fit in among the superficial standards set by society. I thought wearing clothes that didn't scream "outsider" would make me appreciate my existence.

On one scorching summer, I decided to stash away $200 from my mother and go on a little shopping spree for this one time. In my head, I believed it was a fair deal to spend some amount on me from the money I had earned with my blood and sweat; however, my mother was not happy with my decision, and that is when a silent war was born in our small, peaceful abode.

Even though I was working, I was still a child who needed to be loved, but I never received my due share of love, so I decided to walk on a path that was not only different but dangerous for a high schooler. But this is what happens when you leave an underage child unattended—they follow the wrong leads, and that was the case with me as well. So far, all I have received is a mean commentary from my fellow students on my financial status.

I was bullied for repeating my clothes and for having pretty hair, supposedly pushing me to the point from where I found no return. Weeping and sobbing while hiding myself from the eyes of these bullies became a daily ritual for me. It was evident that no teacher, no authority, could stand up for someone like me. They weren't strong enough to protect me, so I started searching for an ally who could shelter me.

In an attempt to run away, I took my first misstep, which led me out of the school's premises, crashlanding onto the merciless streets. Nevertheless, it was still not as big of a crime that I had to be escorted back in a paddy wagon, but the encounter was indeed scary—a reminder that life from home would not be as carefree as it once used to be. Besides that, my need to fit in and the threat of being subjected to extreme bullying made me rely on the wrong alliance. I became a part of those I never imagined I could call my friends—the infamous New York City gang members. This was my attempt to protect myself from the students who openly cursed at authority figures without consequence and did not fear the police.

It was my conscious decision to walk on the edge rather than to live while being circled by high school bullies. As a fifteen-year-old, I did the best I could to survive among the tall buildings. I still do not know when those scary-looking people with each of their stories untold became my shelter from the coldblooded high school bullies, but one thing is clear: if it were not for them, my life at high school would have fallen in the pit of despair long ago.

Chapter 3

"To lose balance sometimes for love is part of living a balanced life."

- Elizabeth Gilbert, Eat, Pray, Love

My teenage years, which in previous chapters were falling to rack and ruin, were now ready to be introduced to the new character of my life. The time had finally arrived when my destiny decided to expose the long-waited plot twist waiting for me in the concrete walls of Queens. During my high school years, I met my counterpart for life, my boyfriend, in the most crowded alley and unexpected way. This was the same man who later added a touch of fiction to my dull reality.

It is the story of when I struggled to find my identity as an individual. Conventionally, I was not perceived as a girl who would bewitch people with her irresistible charm because I had no money to sponsor myself to the salon. From where I belonged, even dining out was a luxury we could not afford; or, let me rephrase it, it was more like an alien concept. At an age when kids talk about hanging out with friends, I had a family waiting for me back at home who were relying on my little income for their survival. However, there came a turn in my life when, in the hallways of my high school, I started gaining confidence in my natural shell, and in no time, people began noticing me even when I did not entertain any superficial beauty standards. They started to acknowledge me, and suddenly, I became the pretty one for the first time in my life.

The attention that I was getting from the opposite gender put me in a position of the spotlight that I did not entirely hate, or to be precise, I liked the feeling of being in the center. During this time, I met this man who became an integral part of my journey. I clearly remember the bright daylight blurring my vision for a second while at the way station. Waiting for the bus was exhausting until I laid my eyes on an ordinary guy who instantly became unordinary for me among the crowds of many. Without any alarms or warnings, this guy entered my scene, introducing himself with a smile as I boarded the bus. The second encounter was yet another hint from the gateway of destiny, where the bus stop served as the platform for our sweet greetings. It was a lovely day when I was waiting for the bus, and he was waving to me, acknowledging my presence. Our third meeting was a little different—a walk home, which later became a significant event in my life as he took a step forward with a question, "Will you be my girlfriend?"

At first, hesitating, I responded with a yes. For him, it seemed certain to me, and he never disproved my opinion. Since day one, he established the fact that he was dating me and disregarded the idea of indulging in mind games like some immature teenagers. He always took a stand for me where necessary and never left me alone, no matter how the situation worsened. As our relationship progressed, my determination to attend the classes improved. For me, he was my ultimate motivation and the sole reason why I wanted to return to the abyss that bullied me until my thoughts became a traumatizing tale.

But my bullies were not ready to subside, and I could see their reflection in every high school wall, making it almost impossible for me to breathe. As time passed, my fear reached the point where it began dictating my actions. Not long after this, I escaped the hostile hallways to avoid the bullies. As a child who lacked the strength to speak, I remember waking up every morning to get ready for school, pretending to enjoy my routine, but that was just an act. I wanted my mother to stay in the dark—I wanted to hide this for as long as I could because what I was facing at school made me feel embarrassed of myself. I used to clock in early in the morning before my classmates and then leave the premises when I saw students approaching. This did not result well, owing to my growing absence from school. The authorities filled out our mailbox with ominous letters, one after another, but thankfully, my mother remained oblivious to the pain I had to endure in high school.

Meanwhile, my boyfriend was becoming more and more concerned about my association with gangs and violence. He urged me to stay in school while disengaging myself from the gang's activities. He feared these activities could threaten me, and before I ended up at a place where it would be impossible for me to return, I should take a step back. He was not a stereotypical boyfriend; I always found him invested in my well-being. He was my reason not to go astray; he positively influenced my life in every possible way.

But as our story progressed, the complexities in our relationship thickened. His mother, who was not fond of me, made sure that her dislike did not go unnoticed. Her disapproval was deeply rooted in colorism, and yet again, I found myself judged not for who I was but for the shade of my skin, pushing me back to the murk of self-doubt as I questioned myself: Am I even deserving of love? But, my boyfriend, who used to protect me from the bullies at the high school, was now standing tall in front of societal prejudice. He made me feel like the most special person in the world, ensuring I received my fair share of love despite his mother's disapproval. He did not leave me just because his mother disapproved of me; he stayed with me until the end. It did not take us long enough to discover that we were expecting our first child right out of high school. I won't lie; parenthood was a daunting challenge for both of us, who were still learning the ways of the world.

As two young souls, we found ourselves stuck under the clouds of uncertainty; however, my partner showed a great example of maturity. Even though we both were equally ignorant about the process and what we should do next, my boyfriend took it upon himself to guide us through the process of confirming the pregnancy. This overwhelming decision connected us to Planned Parenthood, and a simple test revealed the life growing within me. But, for some reason, we both found ourselves more concerned about our families. A child out of wedlock? We all knew the consequences, but we were determined to retaliate if any harm came our way since now it was about our baby. Telling my single mother about the pregnancy was among the most challenging part of this whole process. We were financially unstable, and with limited knowledge of life, I feared her reaction. Yet, despite her initial disappointment, my boyfriend's commitment helped mold her decision. Even this unexpected push for marriage came from her since she had to do something to save the family from the so-called shame. My boyfriend, who was now my husband, took the significant step of delaying a public announcement of my pregnancy, especially announcing to his parents to protect me from any criticism from their end.

It was the auspicious day of Christmas when my daughter bestowed our lives with her presence. Holding her into my arms, I realized for the first time what motherhood was like. My mother-in-law, who loathed my existence, did not accept our baby. The cruelty was she refused to look at her granddaughter. Instead, she accused me of committing infidelity. But I did not fear a thing because my husband stood beside me as my shield.

However, my happiness did not last for long, and just two weeks after our daughter's birth, my husband enlisted in the Navy. We stayed separated for over six long months, and I waited all alone for his return until our daughter was almost seven months old. Ironically, the critiques from my mother-in-law about our daughter's appearance and my alleged affair backfired when she turned out to be the spitting image of her father's side of the family.

While my husband was stationed at a different location, I shared a shed with my mother. It was when I decided to return to my studies to provide a better future for my daughter. At that time, my younger brother chose to stand by my side as we alternated the duty of babysitting my daughter. Undoubtedly, he was my hero! So far, everything was bearable until, at the age of 15, my destiny collided with an unfortunate incident. I usually do not leave my house without offering my prayers, but on that dreading day, I started my day with no mention of my prayers and ended up in a deadly car crash. With no exaggeration intended, I was extracted from the metal wreckage; I had no apparent scars, but internally, I was a mess. I was suffering from internal scars, concussions, and excruciating headaches, and I was constantly in and out of consciousness. The law apprehended the driver, who was sent to the court for a legal battle.

After I turned eighteen, I recall receiving a call from my insurance company suggesting I collect the compensation money. Well, desperate times call for desperate measures, and so, along with my mother, I rushed to the lawyer's office to collect my well-deserved money. Upon stepping into his office, a sudden chill pervaded the air, sending shivers down my spine. It dawned on me that it wasn't merely the office space growing cold but rather the invisible barrier of ice dividing me and my mother, straining our relationship. It became apparent that money, as ever, possessed the power to fracture even the most robust of bonds.

My mother believed the check was rightfully hers and that she deserved a monetary reward for taking me to appointments. And as much as I was grateful for her assistance, I could not let my grip on the cheque be loosened since it was the only way to get a little financial relief. I had to take this decision for my daughter's sake, but my mother was furious by my decision. She made herself clear that I was no longer welcome in her home. Not knowing where to go, I made a desperate call to my husband, who was deployed somewhere far in Virginia. But, no matter how far he was, the distance did not stop him from rescuing me from the face of adversity. He boarded a Greyhound bus right away, and upon his arrival, we left my mother's house in the freezing cold, searching for a place to call our own.

My husband searched for lodging on cold and dark nights, and all I could do was take pity on our situation. Soon after that, we secured a basement apartment where we started rebuilding our lives. As we settled in our new home, my husband returned to Virginia, leaving me and her daughter behind. Three years later, our family expanded with our second child on its way. This was happy news, and I received it with joy, but part of me was anxious since my husband was once again away at sea. It was the time when communication was limited, and the news of my pregnancy reached him after six months. But throughout my second pregnancy, my three-year-old daughter was my strength. She never nagged me when she was starving; she patiently brought a jar of peanut butter and a few slices of bread so I could make her a sandwich.

Now that I have time to recall, those were some stressful days; I feared going into labor all alone. The worst news came when, after a few tests, my doctor projected that my daughter was exhibiting indicators that showed she was suffering from a medical problem. I believed it was a testing time for me, and I immediately resorted to nothing but prayers, knowing God would never let any bad come to me.

As I predicted, on that miraculous day when my daughter was born, the doctor was left baffled when they saw that my newborn daughter showed no signs of the expected medical condition; instead, she was perfectly healthy. That was the day I realized that no matter how alone we think we are, there is always an unseen power—a source above everyone looking after our well-being.

Chapter 4

"The single biggest problem in communication is the illusion that it has taken place."

- ***George Bernard Shaw***

After the arrival of our second baby, my deluded heart was convinced that the plot of our life would now move to its happily ever after. However, during my second pregnancy, the feeling of being forsaken took over my senses.

My husband, who was stationed at a different destination after the birth of my firstborn, could not return home even when he heard that our second baby was due. His grave mistake was answering the call to join the military three weeks after our first one came to the world. Since then, he had only visited us for a brief period, only to be separated from us again and again.

The nature of his job was rather peculiar and demanded him to leave his family behind and be the breadwinner of the house. However, as a young parent responsible for two children, I never had the chance to look at the world from his perspective. I was so lost in my exhausting life that I never wondered how he was slogging away. While striving to provide the best life for his family, he had to carry the weight of not witnessing the most beautiful phases of his children's lives. But when I turn around now and catch glimpses of our past, I appreciate those simple memories of my babies learning to speak and crawl.

But my husband did not have this luxury. Since the day our children came into the world, our story met the moments of separation—not to mention his military obligations were to be blamed here. While carrying my oldest baby, I remember standing on Norfolk's piers, bidding him farewell. It became a ritual sort of thing for my baby and me to see him turn around and leave us with an uncertain future. On that day, standing on the pier, we both were oblivious to what was coming for us. Neither of us could have ever forecast in our wildest dreams that his brief visit would leave such a beautiful present behind. As he departed, our eyes traced his footsteps, a little blurry—a little teary, thinking it would be only two of us now to rely on. But I guess God had something else planned for us as I learned about my pregnancy for the second time. I distinctly remember the day I wrote to my husband about our second child. I felt a series of emotions rush to my brain, my hands trembling with happiness, and all I could think of was informing him about the little angel willing to complete our family.

Those days, telephone conversations were not even a thing, and I had to send him letters personally through the postal service. I had always believed this was the beauty of the time until I realized it took six months for my husband to learn about my second pregnancy. When he returned to us, my second-born was already seven months old, entering the phase of mastering walking. Occasionally, I wondered how he would react while he held the letter in his hand, surrounded by an unfamiliar environment. Would he be happy, gloomy, excited, or numb? What would be his state of mind? After all, he was becoming a father once and again.

Yet, I also believe it must have been heart-wrenching to witness that he had missed the first babbling words of his firstborn, the unstable steps into the world, which were replaced by her walking mastery. The guilt of not being present must have sucked his soul. The fear of leaving his pregnant wife alone might have eaten him from his core, but he was a military man who never showed any signs of vulnerability. He did not allow us to sneak into his heart and observe his pain. Instead, he decided to keep us closer to him, where he could see us frequently. After a while, he moved us to Chicago, where we contended with enough challenges and trials awaited ahead of us.

Chicago was a lonely place where I isolated myself under the huge parasol of its sky. Our family was a young family who met the road to struggle at an early age without any support from a familiar face. Responsibilities weighed down our little existence while we were surrounded by nothing but creepy, estranged people. We moved to an apartment in a completely new neighborhood, yet alienated from the rest of the world. Now, when I think about the time, the booming sound and weird invaders, the spooky residence, and the frightening passersby, they all connect me to the nostalgic memory of my time alone in Chicago.

I stepped into the parental shoes at a young age. My husband was mainly deployed to different places, so I was a single mother taking care of her daughters alone. My husband was always stuck at his work, and his constant deployment never allowed us to spend even a day in peace. But I had gathered the courage for my children—I had to pick up the fragments of my faded youth to provide my babies with everything I could since I was the only one they could depend on. However, the days I had lived before I stepped into motherhood were entirely different from how I live now. I remember the mere act of walking to the grocery store with my child was thick with unease. Walking through narrow alleyways among the eerie strangers did not let me sleep for a wink; every day, I feared the intrusion from external sources. Those were the days I dread to live again!

I had tried and tried to extend my stay in Chicago. We were close to my husband—occasionally, but we got to feel the warmth of his presence there. Moving elsewhere meant leaving him behind, and I was not ready. However, the pounding on the door and the persistent attempt to break into my house scared me for my children's safety. I could not bring myself to stay another night in Chicago while some stranger banged on my door like they would break in anytime soon.

My only resort was to talk to my husband about the situation and move back to New York. In a short time, I plummeted back to the streets of New York. Since the beginning, I knew it was a double-edged sword where I could either save my daughters or my marriage from crumbling down. Putting my faith in our vows together, I returned to my mother in New York. But more than my marriage, this relocation put my relationship with my mother at stake, and my husband had to get me out of her grip quickly. I started living solo again, this time in New York, and felt liberated and scared as I was now responsible for two daughters.

However, my fear was shortly laid out to rest with my husband's sudden return. We settled in Virginia this time, where our family's story found its anchors. With its stability and togetherness, Virginia was the perfect city to raise our children in unison. As a military wife, by now, I had learned to adapt, weather separations, and accept the momentarily moments of togetherness, cherishing the fragments of unity. At the same time, we continued living a nomadic life.

My husband's career choices were the reason behind our numerous deployments, leaving me to shoulder the responsibilities of our home, our kids, and our livelihood. It was a continuous cycle of supporting his career to meet our basic needs.

However, despite providing him with ceaseless support, my life was still filled with a feeling of inadequacy. I always felt hollow—as if a piece of me was missing, but I could never figure out what it was until I realized I lacked independence. Even though I lived in the house from day to night, I had no control over its finances or had no say in any other crucial matters. I felt more like a menagerie kept inside a house because it was the crowning achievement. I was confined to a world where driving myself anywhere or even a simple trip to the grocery store seemed like an unattainable luxury. On top of that, his absence left me isolated while I staggered through parenthood without any friends or the trust to build new connections.

When I returned to New York, I carried a guarded mentality, telling me to stay cautious and hesitant all the time, and the Southern hospitality was too much for me to take. All the greetings and kind gestures made me question the people around me; were they friendly, or was that a pretense? Nonetheless, somewhere, I did yearn for companionship. Even though I was skeptical of letting anyone in, I wanted someone to share my loneliness with me. But the encounters that I had with strangers scared me to the extent that I tightly held on to the shield of alienation, thinking this way, I would save my children.

Days passed by quickly as I eagerly waited for my husband to return while raising two young children. No matter how exhausting and draining my routine was, my eyes always stayed on the door, waiting for his arrival. During one of these periods, I reconnected with an acquaintance from my past, someone I knew from my New York days. Strangely, the geographic distance had never allowed our bond to flourish before, but circumstances had shifted. Her relocation to Virginia was similar to my journey as a wife, creating a bridge for us to connect. I heard my voice for the first time in a while—I heard myself speaking, giggling, and sharing my worries as if I had known this person for a long time.

To this day, I regret letting my guard down around her and letting her inside my safe home. I could have never predicted how much risk this newly discovered friendship could pose at my warm, cozy home.

Dressed as a friend, she started questioning my husband's absence on the first day. She bombarded me with doubts and skepticism, pointing out the threat that was attached to the nature of my husband's job. But the situation worsened when her words started making sense to me. My friend's piercing questions went straight to my heart and made me suspicious of my husband's fidelity even though we never had concrete proof against him.

Before I met her, the thought of my husband committing infidelity had never crossed my mind. I have always believed that our marriage was formed on the pillars of truth, which no power could destroy. But, suddenly, the illusion of a perfect marriage was shattered, and unsettling thoughts substituted it that I had never before entertained.

Despite the doubts surrounding every corner of my consciousness, life continued. Each return of my husband gave hope to my already crumbling marriage. We fell back into our routines, never daring to question the circumstances, even as cracks began to surface. Loneliness often spellbound my thoughts, and my husband's absence from my life further added to my misery. I yearned to be heard, and the only person who landed me an ear was this friend of mine who took advantage of my loneliness. Initially, her presence provided me with a breathing space. Yet, her strong influence on me ruined the peace of our marriage.

My husband's life as a sailor meant that he had to be separated from his family for God knew how many days. With restricted communication and no means to contact him in an emergency, I allowed the seed of doubts to take its foundation within me.

In my innocence, I also accepted this as the norm and waited for his return as if all military wives shared the same fate. The small circle in which I was living was my safe sphere. I always felt that I belonged within the four walls, and the radiation of my children's smiles was all that I cared for.

Once again, we moved closer to his job in Virginia, but this time, we moved to a house that truly belonged to us. Around this time, my husband started anchoring more to the land, and where his frequent returns did add joy to our family, I started observing my place in the family.

What was I becoming? A mere caretaker of the house or just a trophy wife roaming around uselessly? My husband had all the finances under his control. He decided the day for grocery shopping and the bills, and all I did was stand with him when he was giving commands. I never realized that I was being controlled in this marriage—I never looked at our life from this lens. All I ever cared about was the children, the family, and my husband, and I believed that my only role was to be the house administrator. I was oblivious to the subtle manipulations creeping into my perceptions, but when I started scrutinizing his actions, my views on my husband and our perfect marriage started changing.

A year or two into our marriage, the strain of finances caused cracks in our relationship. As the burden of financial constraints intensified, the exterior of contentment dissolved, exposing the fault lines of control and manipulation that had been hidden all along this time. Frustration started controlling my rationality, and so often, I began asking him about his whereabouts and the supposed adultery.

His constant absence from the house made me skeptical about his extramarital affair and also instilled a sense of insecurity within me. I was deprived of his attention and always resentfully thought, *okay, I'm not getting that attention; I'm not getting his quality time*. I was so exhausted that I failed to see his story.

I only cared about the expenses and where he was spending the money. My insecurity got to the point that I began to think that the reason he had an affair was because he no longer felt I was attractive.

I wanted him to need me; I was yearning to receive attention from his end, but he never had time for me. Instead, I started feeling like I was never good enough for him. I felt it was a compromise until I stepped outside my tiny sphere with my friends and received a barrage of praise for my appearance. It was a bliss to receive compliments from strangers, knowing I still had it in me. On that day, I was riding high on happiness, not knowing that it was the opening move that would destroy what was supposed to be my happily ever after.

Chapter 5

"There are all kinds of ways for a relationship to be tested, even broken, some, irrevocably; it's the endings we're unprepared for."

- ***Katherine Owen***

As I woke up that day, alone in my bed, surrounded by my children, I wondered what I had become. Was I born to be a wife, a daughter, or a mother, or did I have a role beyond these conventional woman-centric duties? I was the lady of the house, but that was all. I was the grand title holder, but what was the meaning behind my existence? Something constantly piqued me to question my individuality—Have I ever been my own person?

My life took a bizarre turn during my husband's deployment. When loneliness corrupted my brain, I befriended a girl whose life choices shimmered from a distance. She was the woman who preferred to live with misleading allure in the semi-darkness of her existence. Similar to my life, she had a family waiting at home, yet she lived a promiscuous lifestyle. At the same time, I stayed within my caged reality, whose door was left open, but I had to cater to my children, and so, I waited like a widow for the return of my husband. I had no autonomy over myself, and even my mind was partially controlled by my doting husband. My God is my witness; I never permitted an ounce of skepticism for him. I have always believed in his love and loyalty and never doubted him until I met this girl.

Nevertheless, as the nights started getting longer, my days became haunted by his longing, and my heart reached its maximum capacity. The feeling of emptiness, the overwhelmingness that had taken over me, bore me down with every passing moment. Besides that, the person I befriended started planting the seed of doubt into my already trampled soul. Occasionally, she would claim the idea of my husband cheating on me and that the extended ship hours were a cover-up to veil his infidelity. For a long time, I refused to let her words penetrate me, but as time passed, her trap of utterings started making sense to me. What if he was playing with my loyalty? I was not there with him, and I could not catch him in the act. Maybe he had taken advantage of this opportunity. All her words that intoxicated my brain left a deep scar on my heart. I remember not being angry, not being furious but hurt. I feared the day when her words would come true. How would I face the reality?

I know I should have trusted my husband—the man who did so much for our family but the situation I was stuck in at that time made me forget all his kindness. The time we had spent was limited, and the time he had stayed at the ship outweighed my trust in him. His absence was as long as the nights of December, and by now, I had started to forget who he was as a person. I could not tell if all the manipulation from my so-called friend's end was accurate or if it was just an attempt to ruin my relationship with my husband. Still, this dimwitted individual was unaware of the damage gradually being done.

After a while, my husband returned from deployment, and my world, which had now found attention from elsewhere, was suddenly stuck between morality and individuality. The dilemma was a lot for me to take as I discussed the storm hidden behind me with my neighborhood companion. My companion laughed and encouraged me to leave my worries behind the closed doors of home. She invited me to go out with her into the nightlife. At first, it was my curiosity that led me there. I was a teen mom who practically never got to live a life of her own. Not that it was anyone's fault or that I despised my current living conditions, but part of me desired to live an ordinary life, leaving the baggage behind.

The nights were surreal, with dimly lit bars and nightclubs as our stage. Lost in the moment, I did not realize what I was getting myself into. The nightclub made me forget the image of me as a mother, and a sense of wholeness took over me. I felt this place answered my question; here I was, living my life while being my own person.

My friend's outfit selection usually drew a lot of attention. But that evening, a mysterious man emerged from the club's shadowy corners. He was a tall, handsome stranger who became the focal point of the evening at Hammerheads. His presence seemed magnetic, and I felt a peculiar but undeniable connection at that moment. My senses were dimed as I observed him coming my way. Against the music and laughter, he singled me out—not my eminent friend but me. His gaze locked onto mine as he took a few steps closer.

I could not forget this extraordinary night when someone's attention departed from my friend, and an unusual spotlight intensely illuminated my life. This stranger, whose charisma was impossible to ignore, sparked a flame of intrigue within me. He was mysterious and well-known; he was quiet yet heard. He was lost but connected to his roots. He looked more like myself, utterly detached from reality but existing in the moment. If truth be told, I could not tell if that was his reality or my illusions, but the feelings I held for him at that time were more than real.

Time to time, when I think about it, I wonder if I regret meeting my friend. Did I want to disappear from the night at the club? Maybe, but do I regret meeting him? Absolutely not! I do not intend to rue the time spent with him even if the guilt crept over me and consumed me entirely.

As the dusk began advancing, this captivating stranger handed me his contact information, leaving me anxious about his gesture. A mother of two accepting his gratitude—was that really something to be mortified of? It was not a crime to desire a genuine companion. I was tired of being married and living a dowager life. Yet, my marriage seemed like a big show where my husband never lent an ear—he never paid attention to my worries. But this stranger ignited my long-dead desire to be heard. It was an unconventional encounter that left me questioning the boundaries of my fidelity. I battled between ethics and yearnings. I knew that if I took one more step, I would never be able to go home and maintain my motherly dignity.

But anyway, I found myself using a friend's phone to make that one call, and he answered quickly, acknowledging the pleasure of our meeting. His reaction was weird for me since I was not habitual of random phone calls, but as the night settled within me, I thirsted to maintain a stable connection with him. However, it seemed like a far-fetched dream as I had never shared my number with him, and the phone I used to call him never belonged to me. What a pity it was! Deep somewhere, I began thinking maybe I lost my only hope of reviving myself from the dead.

Days passed, and I found myself occupied in his thoughts. My neighborhood friend also knew the queer feeling that took over me. She knew it would receive respite nowhere but in his presence.

Fast forward a few months, and my friend unearthed the identity of this secret man from the nightclub. I described him as someone whose beauty could lead you astray, and I was not imprecise while drawing his imagery. But even as a married lady, I shouldn't have allowed such an idea even to cross my head subtly, but suddenly adultery took hold of my thoughts.

The memory of that night remained with me, and believe me, if I ever got the chance to turn back the time and return to that night, I would have indeed done that. Although giving in to the temptation was not the best choice, it could not be helped.

Despite my commitment to family and loyalty, the seeds of doubt that my friend planted within me gave me an easy pass to act on impulse. I was envious of my husband's carefree adventures, which put me in unrest. It became a part of my routine to question my life, "Why am I home-bound while he explores the world?" But hear me out: I refuse to justify my acts—I cannot shield them. Even though I briefly lost all sense of right and wrong, I knew one thing for sure: my actions were not justified.

Nonetheless, I can vouch that my loyalty to my husband remained intact even after the harmless conversation between that stranger and me. I would not lie; there was a subtle shift in my notion of life, but the thought of abandoning my current life to start a new one never stroked me. I was off the right track; I accept that, but I never dared to think about leaving my family, which is my truth.

Three months later, when my life started returning to normal, my friend meddled, connecting me with the mysterious man from the nightclub. She mentioned that a mutual friend of hers is acquainted with this guy, and he worked for him. For a moment, it felt like a lucid dream where I could not differentiate my reality. But, as excitement brimmed over me, I realized it was no dream but a decision made by destiny.

I received his contact information from my friend and tried contacting him, but this time, it was from my phone. Our conversations flowed effortlessly, as if we always knew each other, while guilt got lost in thin air. I knew I was not doing anything wrong; it was a plain, platonic conversation that would hurt none. As time passed, our brief discussion extended to long hours of conversation where we talked about God. His calm voice added composure to my messed-up routine.

I recall the day when he invited me to a football match. The initial fear of meeting him made me ponder whether I should politely decline his offer or let my guts dictate my path. And the moment my friend learned about my dilemma, she encouraged me and pushed me to attend the football game. *Safety in numbers,* I thought, as I asked her to tag with me. She, along with another friend, happily accompanied us to the match.

Our first meeting was casual and innocent, but it opened the door for a deeper connection. Whenever I had a brutal fight with my husband, I longed to see him and to run to him. In my most vulnerable phase, my thoughts wandered and surrounded his presence. I was not even somewhat guilty for my actions, but this one small argument with my husband catalyzed re-evaluating my true sentiments.

Looking back, I realized I found myself using a trivial argument as an excuse to justify my act. My sudden arrival at his place, given that vulnerability, stayed with me, was unreasonable. It was the night I tumbled into the arms of another man. I received warmth and love from him that I had not experienced before. But the fact that my family was waiting for me back home had evaded my mind till then. The soothing feeling—the unfamiliar emotions left me perplexed, unable to comprehend my feelings and thoughts. When I returned home, guilt consumed me, and I had no clue how I would be facing my husband.

In that moment of self-reflection, I questioned my actions. I catechize the purity of our relationship. I regret every bit of the deed as a sense of brokenness suffocated me. How did such a strong bond lead me down this path?

As the breadwinner of our household, my husband was fighting his battles, and look at how I chose to repay his efforts. The guilt was consuming me, and I needed an outlet to hear the crime I had committed. One day, soon after, my friend visited me and started weeping over her broken ties with her boyfriend. As she shared her secret sitting on my dining table, part of me coaxed me to reveal what was burdening me. So, I confided in her, only to face an uncalled threat. The complexities of her failed relationship transformed her into a blackmailer, ready to expose my wrongdoing.

I still could not believe my friend had laid down a warning to reveal my misdemeanor to my husband just because her relationship was broken beyond repair. But the reality was that if not her, someone else would have used my truth against me—if not today, then some other day, I had to choose between speaking my truth and preserving my marriage. Stuck between the war of brain and mind, I decided to come clean.

As I sat my husband down, I poured out the ugly truth while expressing remorse for my actions. The guilt in my eyes reflected the aches of my soul. I was grief-stricken, and anybody present at that moment could have understood my position. Perhaps this was why my husband's reaction did not meet anger but forgiveness. He heard me and took his time to process the situation. He knew infidelity was not in my blood. I was wrong but not unfaithful by nature.

When he was ready to move forward, I decided to sever ties with the person involved. The account of my infidelity was revoked then and there. His calmness that weighed my heart told me to devote myself to him for eternity, and I was ready for it. The thought of causing him further pain was unbearable for me now.

My husband and I chose to start over, and I was able to forgive myself as he had. We decided to leave our past behind and move to a new location where no one would ever remind us of what had gone wrong.

Chapter 6

"The truly scary thing about undiscovered lies is that they have a greater capacity to diminish us than exposed ones. They erode our strength, our self-esteem, our very foundation."

- Cheryl Hughes

His silence allowed me to comprehend what was said when the words struggled to deliver their true essence. Deceiving him was out of the question. I wanted to seal the cracks of our relationship—I wanted us to become the perfect couple we once used to be. So, while clutching the desire to bring everything back to its place, we took a leap of faith and moved to a new location or, precisely, an entirely new continent.

To be honest, it was our frail attempt to revive what I had buried alive, and I believed it was my chance to bring happiness back to our cozy household. I was willing to go to any extent to fill my children's and their father's lives with hues and bloom. For the most part, my husband was also determined to leave everything behind us. We assured each other that we would live a life where deception would never find its way toward us.

I was grateful for his kindness and composure, but the quietness of the surroundings was killing me from the inside. His silence was haunting; why did he not question my love for him? I pondered if a storm inside him was making his place or if it was the ordinary behavior of a sailor who spent more time cruising than understanding his family matters. As I shrugged my thoughts, I promised never to inflict any harm upon this man again. I vowed to endure the battles of our relationship and withstand the harshness of life, no matter how deadly it got. I wanted to provide him with the ultimate comfort and add happiness to his life, which became my motto. Every day, I woke up excited about the better prospects awaiting us.

Having said that, relocating to a new place was about escaping my past and experiencing life in a way I had never imagined. I had always felt that journey was significant for our relationship since it was initiated on the foundation of truth. It unfolded the phase of our marriage that I never knew existed before.

Years passed, and the illusion of a perfect marriage in which I was living so far started to wither away. While relocating, I did not consider life's complexities and how they could break the strongest of the relationship. Perhaps life had not revealed its ugliest side yet, or maybe I refused to understand. But the truth was, a new continent did not guarantee more attention from my husband. He still had a life other than ours, and my world revolved around him. Vacations with my children were the only times that poured moments of solitude into my life.

While on vacation and away from him, I never allowed another seed of doubt to form in my head. I put my trust in him, knowing he had never once mentioned my infidelity since that unfortunate day. However, when I look back, I believe his interactions were not free from his red flags. Yet, it was me who failed to see through them. His association with other females, the shady interactions, and the nuances of his movements were subtle signals I chose to ignore.

Despite the brewing undercurrents, I believed in his sincerity. Blindfolded by the weight of my past wrongdoings, I believed what he showed on the surface level was the entire truth, dismissing the tiniest space for any suspicions to dribble. In a little while, happiness started evading our house. With every passing day, little arguments swamped our peaceful relationship, quietly hinting at the misfortune that was about to suck the joy out of my house. Soon, the scene of vulnerability started setting the stage as his anger began taking a new form.

As we moved to the United States, his narrative of the verbal abuse became apparent. It was as if our already broken relationship was once again hit by the tip of the iceberg, ready to turn into tiny fragments. The geographical distance that once absorbed our disagreements reappeared, forcing me to conceal my raw emotions behind the mask of bravery. Before long, the mere verbal fights also transformed into bitter clashes where I was once again held accountable for my past infidelity.

The bitter conflicts marked by resentment made me completely silent; what else could have been done there? I committed a grave sin that haunted my existence. He would occasionally use our shared past as a weapon to stab me in the face and accuse me of more and more things, but I would always accept his attacks because, for once, I dared to doubt myself.

In an attempt to protect what we had, I thought he chose to forgive me so we could move forward. That was not his intention. He held me captive; he made me a prisoner of my thoughts. My head found his act suspicious, but my heart fooled me by saying maybe he was madly, deeply in love. After all, I was the mother of his children—I filled his existence with these two precious beings. But, no! That was just my delusional self speaking. He was guilty of not being honest with me, not of being blinded by my love, which is why I wasn't pardoned. I reflected the same image in him as he did in me; his pride was the only thing that separated us.

The conflict continued to take a drastic turn as suspicions crept into my mind. An eerie thought seeped into my brain: what if I was never forgiven, but it was merely a pretense? Now, I was standing on the edge of returning to my family or running away from the shame. The choice had to be mine, so I decided to give in and devote myself, even if that meant staying away from my husband.

Then came the day when my husband came to me and shared the plans for his next deployment. He revealed that his deployment required him to stay away from the family for three years. It was not an easy choice, and we both knew somewhere that this might serve our familial ties, but anyway, I wanted to prove to him that I was standing by his side. Strange, but I was involved in this choice, purely driven by the desire to provide stability for our children. I wanted my children to befriend people who would stay with them for many years, even when we departed this world, but the constant deployment did not allow them to form a bond with anyone.

The decision was not without sacrifice, for my husband willingly chose a deployment to Afghanistan in the wake of the 9/11 events. He knew it was life-threatening, but something, some unknown powers, called for him, and I guess he ended up following the footsteps that led him to ruin us as a family. During those times, Afghanistan was no less than a combat zone where all the attempts to communicate were in vain. In addition to that, my husband had to undergo rigorous training to prepare for the circumstances approaching them. Yet, amidst everything, I used to wait to hear his voice while he made calls from unknown numbers of some female acquaintance he barely knew. I remember asking him to provide me with a way to connect to him so that at least I knew he was well and alive, but there was no way I could contact him—not even on the numbers he had called from.

To my surprise, before entering the combat zone, my husband briefly visited our home. His guilt probably told him to see his children's faces, or maybe it was the fear of this being his last chance to meet them because life never came with an apparent expiry. Whatever the reason was, his sudden arrival added the elements of joy to our gloomy routine. I was happy to see my family united after such a long time until I heard the voice of this strange woman. In the dead of night, one such call shattered my trust into bits and pieces. As I picked up the phone, I realized the voice on the other end belonged to a woman, a stranger who knew intimately about my husband's life. I wondered who she could be—an acquaintance or something more than that. Nonetheless, my brain did not have to overthink for long as she decided to carry on with the revelations, spilled like bitter tea.

Broken but conscious, I demanded confrontation from my husband, learning his truth was my right. Even though I could have approached him with a preconceived notion, I let him speak for himself.

As time threw us into the combat zone of life, my husband begged for forgiveness, and I, in turn, granted it willingly. Once again, the weight of my past wrongdoings bore me down, and I halted myself from demanding any more justification. I thought I was not the right person to question his actions, knowing well enough that I was never caught in the act; instead, I chose to put my secret in the open because I respected our relationship. God knew since when he was trying to deceive us, but that was never my intention. I went astray once but returned shortly to whom I belonged, but what about him? Had he even considered returning for the sake of our children? I was devastated to learn that he visited his girlfriend in California while my eyes were stuck on the threshold, wondering whether he had his first meal of the day.

After he went to a combat zone, contacting him became another harrowing journey. Months and months passed, but no clue would connect me to him. I was stranded once again with my thoughts, and all I remembered was to console myself and believe he was alive; he was living well. A year of no communication pushed our happily married life into mistrust as our conversations were reduced to silence.

My once devoted heart was now ready to drop. I was tired of this everyday skepticism, and my body felt exhausted as if I was involved in arduous manual labor. But even then, part of me longed to hear his voice, ensuring that he was sound and safe.

When my husband returned from the battleground, the relief took over me. I did not question him about his disappearance; I did not ask him why a phone call was such a demanding task for him. I was happy to know that he returned unscathed—no injuries, no visible scars—just the tales and experiences he had gathered on the roads of Afghanistan. My concern for his safe return diminished all the doubts and worries I had held before, and in that fleeting moment, all seemed well. However, his behavior was drastically harsh toward children, and he barely formed any bond with us. He was always grumpy and held a dark aura around him, making me think it was the aftereffects of his last deployment.

But this was not my husband's permanent residence per our fate, and who could have stood against destiny? My husband was called once again for another deployment, with a promise to abandon his family a thousand times.

But something about this deployment was different; my hunch could not lie to me. Indeed, it had to be something special for my husband to sail outside the United States without discussing it with me. The distance between us widened as we never found each other on the same page.

Accusations and blame were his weapons of choice, projecting his internal Warfield onto me. He used the ancient history of my extra-marital affair and clung to the betrayal. Every day, he tried to paint me as an antagonist who mercilessly broke his trust, but he was nowhere to be accountable. The last time he visited us before the deployment, his rage erupted within him, throwing the tranquility out of our home.

The sound of breaking items made me fear him. He was never like this; what took over him? The PTSD or aftereffects—I could not justify his toxicity anymore. I rushed to the restroom and hid myself behind the locked room. His post-combat mental state was never justified. What happened that day shook me to the core.

Time seemed to have stopped for me as I dreaded his existence. Shortly, he received another call for deployment, and this time, Japan became his haven for nearly a decade, where we both lived apart and never tried to reach out to each other. The unsaid separation period began, and the distance between us reflected where we stood as a couple.

Chapter 7

"Absence is a house so vast that inside you will pass through its walls and hang pictures on the air."

- Pablo Neruda

My husband's infidelity, his constant abuse, and my need to protect my kids from his dark shadow forced me to take drastic steps due to his regression in behavior. After my husband's departure to Japan, my life turned ironic and threw me back to where I came from—the streets of New York City. The presumed separation had already shoved me into darkness. At that point, I assumed the city's lightning might give a startling touch to my life. But what I did not predict was the bitter reality that I was compelled to see.

My family, who resided at a mere ten-minute ride from my house, found themselves tied up in their monotonous routine, and here I was, brawling with my life about my crumbling state. Days turned into night, and as I crawled back into my shell, I found loneliness at the other end, waiting desperately to consume me.

In the initial days, I regretted moving to New York, but my only intention was to familiarize my children with what a happy family looked like. So far, they had witnessed a life where instability embossed its mark deeply on their innocence, and I wanted to provide them with nothing but love. But, even the bustling roads of New York failed to offer much. Nonetheless, I figured it was a great place to learn what abandonment was. At first, I questioned myself: what would it be like if I had not chosen to move back and instead accompanied my abusive husband? Perhaps the unsaid separation would have been revoked by then. But what I forgot then was the fact that he willingly chose to deceive me. He did not commit a mistake but had a full-fledged affair on the side while his wife yearned to see him once.

I started befriending loneliness in the crowded city, the only companion who crept into my solitary hours. The truth was that my family no longer wanted to be a part of my suffering, or at least this is what I felt at that time. I was the forsaken one who desperately craved a genuine connection. Perchance, heaven heard my pleas from miles away, and a childhood friend entered my life as an antidote to my loneliness at that moment. We were from the same country and shared the same culture and values. He had the glow that could light my world; he was the warmth my cold heart needed the most.

Our encounter was simple, yet it made me feel as if life had mainly arranged a reunion so we would not lose hope in love. It was the call of fate to turn this childhood friend into a soulmate. The more our paths intersected, the easier it became to see why he was placed in my world. He was the missing piece of my puzzle; he soon became one of us without having to put in much effort. He had an affectionate gaze and loved to roam around the kitchen as if it was his passion. He did not shy away from the chores and stayed present beside me in the form of flesh and as a kind supporter. Unlike my ex-husband, who was now becoming a part of my past, this man preferred to live in the moment. Believe me when I say it did not take much time for me to reconnect with him; he gave me the security I had always yearned for, or else I would not have let him hold my children in his arms.

Our relationship must have been born from the ashes of my dead dreams, but now it was standing on the blooming ground for my happiness. The fact that my family knew him was a plus. They accepted him and loved his presence while I beheld the image of our future.

I would not lie; alienation and lonesomeness could bring down the strongest warrior, and lacking genuine human communication, I was shattered to the core before I met him. The feeling of being lost and vulnerable began taking over me gradually, but this childhood friend provided me with the will to live. We pushed our relationship to fill the space created by the absence of familiar faces in a frantic attempt to preserve a real connection.

My children had yearned to find someone who would genuinely be loyal to them, and they were the reason I could find some comfort in an old friend. Is this not what I have always feared? I took extreme actions to provide my children with a real connection; I wanted them to stay close to their roots, but look at them now. Their mother was the only person they had by their side, while their connection with their father was weakening.

Their father's once-in-a-year visits painted a picture of emotional detachment among the naïve minds of my daughters. They could not discern why but knew something had changed long ago. Their father barely spent time with them and always carried the harshness in his heart. The father, who once held a special place in their lives, was now transformed into a mere silhouette. It was a bitter pill to swallow that he was physically present, but emotionally, he had shunned his senses for his one and only family. I wondered what exhausted him so much that he started despising the sound of his children calling upon him.

It was a troubled stint for my eldest daughter, who, amid the chaos, was making her way toward the storm of adolescence, augmented by her father's growing distance. In her search for her own self, she sought identity in the most unnerving places, while her attitude highlighted the need to be heard. The pain that she had to encounter as the eldest daughter made her choose a way that was slightly different from the conventional role of children. Additionally, the apparent hormonal changes and the rough upbringing collided with the constant absence of her father from the position of guardian, inflicting an emotional toll on our already fragile existence.

As previously said, my husband only cared about arguments during that phase. It was as if he returned home to take out his frustration over me and the children so that he could move on with his life. It was his defensive stance, or maybe that is how he tackled life so far, but I remember how his worsening attitude only pushed us away. Our family, which was once an intact unit, was into fragments, with each member sustaining hidden injuries from the damage.

Soon, my husband took another deployment, far from our home. His departure to Japan marked the beginning of the end of our twenty-two-year marriage.

Time began to pass very quickly as his rare visits became non-existent. I could sense from a mile that we were finally in the same boat after being married for more than two decades. Love from his end was long gone, and our once-cherished path was now ready to diverge into two. However, what gripped my heart most was how he decided to serve the ties. It was a sure deal that our marriage was on the edge of crumbling; however, this disconnection from me was not the demise of his relationship with our daughters, who needed him the most. He could have chosen to be present with them as their father, but no, he had his priorities straight. He was clever in removing any barrier to his promiscuous living standard. And so, Japan and Hawaii were the accurate places that provided him escapism from the responsibilities that once bound him to our children and me.

You must be wondering how I was even acquainted with his promiscuity. It did not take me long to learn about his countless casual relationships with other women. While I was still grieving over our separation, I received hundreds of calls from his ladies, and each voice pierced through my heart.

As time passed, I learned to live through the almost impossible things to bear. But the day I checked my mailbox and found a letter from the court waiting for me to open up, I lost my stability for a while. The morning was not so bad when a bearer of a cruel decree delivered divorce papers right in front of my house. It contained a document signed in ink, instructing us to grieve over the broken remnants of our sacred union. I wonder how numb I may have been for my eyes to stay dry at that moment. Indeed, emotions engulfed me in a twinkling of sight, but did I have the time to sob and weep?

My existence had been nothing but that of a trophy wife who stayed indoors for years. I was always at the mercy of a man's dependency, and now, when I knew no road toward my survival, I was forsaken by my very husband to fight for me and my children's survival. For years, he made me live in a cage where I had no job and no independence to run as an individual, and he was well aware of my reality. He was the one who snatched my freedom away from me at an early age, but his actions showed he had no remorse for how he chose to destroy me.

I promised myself, as a mother of two, that I would not allow my kids to starve to death. My survival instinct kicked in at that moment, and I knew I needed to adapt to this life before it was too late, for no knight in shining armor would come. It was almost impossible for me to fathom the situation. I was being penalized for his mistakes, but the fact that his life was safe and mine was in danger of being lost made me grin. The only way to promise the world to my children was by ensuring that I remained in this tumbled marriage till he returned to the U.S.A. It was a matter that should be dealt with within the U.S. jurisdiction, and he had to be here for that.

At the time of the separation, one revelation over another was dumped over me. I learned the truth about his multiple families through random ladies. Even though we were standing at a junction where anything was expected of this man I once loved, knowing about his children outside our family put me in a daze. Those were the vows we took together; he told me never to have children with random people, but look at his audacity. He became the reason why our marriage was disrespected in an utterly absurd way. It broke my children; it made them hate their father while I stood there devastated, wondering why my daughters had to go through all this.

Chapter 8

"You may remain a couple after betrayal and even establish a quality relationship, but the mental anguish never leaves, and your soul will haunt you forever."

- RJ Intindola

It was no less than a pleasure for me to burn myself and turn into ashes than to live a life where all I received was betrayal and pain, surprisingly, by the people closest to me. Believe me when I say I was a strong mother who could have witnessed everything, but that is what makes life scary; it breaks even the strongest.

Apart from being a mother, daughter, and someone's wife, I was a human who found solace nowhere in her life. I was backstabbed and left on a trail, alone to die, and you know what was the dreading part? I was not pushed from the cliff by a stranger, but by my people—the people I called love, created a situation where I had no other option but to wait for death to approach me. But even death never favored me. It betrayed me in the name of courage and mocked my destiny when it should have relieved me from this pain.

I was the unfortunate person who never received her share of love, even when all I had to offer in return was love. I was the sort of person who was used by every person I trusted, but they never returned half of what they owed me. However, I never stopped giving what little I had left for me; I never stopped believing that one day, love would find me on the most unexpected eve; perhaps that was why I entrusted my life to the hands of a person who became the reason behind my sorrow.

When my life met its dead end after my marriage crumbled, I confided in that one companion of fifteen years, thinking he would never inflict pain on me. He knew me as a child; he grew up with me with a heart that was not corrupted; above all, he witnessed my aches, so tell me, how could I not trust his vows? We had spent time together in the streets of our hometown, wandering while not caring about the world, but then life drifted apart, and we were connected to the people who became a significant part of our lives.

But funny enough, we were brought together, through complete coincidence after decades, to fill each other's cracks. We sealed our woes and made way for lightning to take over darkness. We sang and shared the same passion. We discussed the culture and faced adversity together, wondering how beautiful this bond was. What started from infatuation turned into love, but it was too pure for me to force a tag on it. Maybe that was why even he decided not to put a label on what we had. It was unnamed, but its sentiments were far more beautiful than any conjugal bond.

I wonder how naïve I had to be to believe in crap like this; how bad was I manipulated that I did not catch his red flags when he subtly refused to give a name to our relationship? He gaslighted me into thinking that this was what I wanted, and I, a victim of infidelity, had not shown even one ounce of skepticism. He had the privilege of being my companion for twelve years, so I refused to doubt his intention. I was constantly wary of him and worried that something as basic as my saying something would make him uncomfortable. I would have never wanted to taint the beautiful relationship that stemmed from our friendship, so I cherished the bare minimum that he offered.

The infatuation morphed into love, which was a pretend from his end, and silly me thought I finally received the love I pleaded with God. I was fresh out of a broken marriage and did not know how to cure my broken heart when I met him for the first time. My emotions intensified as the need to let someone fill my void grew more prominent.

The cracks of a crumbled marriage wanted to be sealed, and in desperation, I refused to see what little effort he was offering me. The memory I made with my ex-husband slipped away from my hand, and this person appeared to be the antidote to our bitter end. However, the void-filling journey soon turned out to be worse than the actual pain that I had yet to heal from. This new person brought experiences and behaviors alien to my world, throwing me at a place where I had to measure my self-worth constantly.

At first, his attitude toward me was a little less suspicious. He was kind to me and loved by my mother, but as time passed, he became a new person that none of us had encountered before. He was no longer the guy I fell in love with but an intruder who would never return my calls but shamelessly come to my house late at night as if he had no better place to sleep.

My house became a resting spot for him, and his intrusion became bar escapades almost every night. Frequently, he started getting into my house uninvited, as late as 5 in the morning, knowing that his routine could pollute my children's innocence. Apparently, he did not see anything wrong with his late-night intrusion and never tried to understand my concern. Still, as a mother, I defended against this behavior and protected my children from the intrusion, for it violated the standards I held dear. Setting a boundary was not a child's play for me. I had never been put in a situation like this before, so I had no clue how to restrict his access to my house, but I had to take a stand since it was a matter of my and my children's safety that should not be compromised at any cost.

As our relationship progressed, I realized this relationship had a series of adversities waiting to break me. Nonetheless, I was not a person who would run away when life got bitter. I knew how much sacrifice it took for the communion of two people, and I was willing to go to any extent to protect my love. Even when his mother constantly blamed me for her son's immature habits, I learned to stay quiet.

Without knowing me, she painted a distorted version of manipulation and deception. She accused me of ruining her son and being the reason behind his frequent club visits, even though I never had a say in it. I, in turn, had to prove my worth to him and his mother, who failed to recognize her son and understand the essence of who I was. Instead of taking responsibility for her son's actions, she held me accountable for the things I had no control over, and I stood there justifying my position. I was a mother—an adult, yet here I was, trying to earn a spur from the mother of the guy who was least bothered by this drama. He was too busy living his own life to be concerned about how his mother's offensive comments were ruining my self-respect.

Our relationship worsened when our conversations switched from in-person to phone calls. Suddenly, I was in a long-distance relationship, and the complexities started haunting me. I was the wife of a man who betrayed her with another woman, yet when I entered my new relationship, I ceased the power to doubt my partner and took an oath to trust him utterly. I had no intention of being perceived as a woman with paranoia who projected her insecurities onto her partner, so I closed my eyes and allowed my heart to take the lead. But occasionally, I wonder if it was the right decision. However, it did not take long enough to realize that trusting a man was the biggest mistake I had ever committed.

A little while into our relationship, I found traces of his other women. At that point, he was staying in the USA; all we had was phone calls to hear one another; that, too, became the medium that brought his dark truth to light and made me see how big of a fool he made out of me. He knew my ex-husband's infidelity bruised my soul, and all my scars were the consequence of cheating, yet he chose the same road to pierce a dagger into my heart. For the second time, I asked the same questions I had left behind: what value did I have for him? Was I just another toy like his previous side chicks?

The realization was gut-wrenching, yet I had none to turn to as usual. I had to survive that storm, for my children needed me. I had to compose myself and understand the bitter truth; it reflected my lack of value in his eyes, and I could never forget it. The man who was supposed to heal me left me shattered and broken, and you look at my hopelessness; he was so far away that I could not even grab him by his collar and ask—Why did you enter my life to ruin the companionship between the two childhood buddies?

The distance, when it seeped into our relationship, filled our days with arguments and turned our nights into a sobbing session where he never cared whether I bawled or unlived myself; all that mattered to him was the peace that he was protecting after ruining mine. He could not endure the traces of joy on my face and had to control every aspect of my life, even if that meant counting my breath. It was clear that the foundational trust I thought existed between us was built on shaky ground.

He always had the urge to control my life, and the moment he realized he could have the controller of my life in his hand, he started manipulating me in a way that he became the ultimate regime while I subverted as a mere human born to commit mistakes. He never mentioned a word out loud, but the constant push and pull from his end highlighted my importance in his life. It was evident that, in his eyes, I deserved no love. He manipulated me into thinking that I was incapable of performing a simple task and that I should never touch a thing as if I had cursed destiny. He restricted my worldview to grey and white while his life remained full of colors with women on his side. He ensured that I never trusted my instincts and conditioned me to think in a way that I began agreeing with every bit of his commands. He made me lose my senses so that I could not detect his eeriness.

This man loved the idea of portraying me as a child since infantilizing me would have benefitted him only. It was a trap to snatch my individuality, and to do so, he continued gaslighting me. Truth be told, to some extent, I did allow him to infantilize me, believing that it was his love language. However, while dwelling on this phase, I failed to recall how hard I had struggled to assert my individuality. I had to fight the battles to become what I was; how could I ever let him cage me when I was born to fly?

Nonetheless, it was too late to mend the brokenness as our relationship was no longer a beautiful tale; instead, it became a chronology of the battlefield—a ledger recording the intensity of my every scar.

The initial sweetness had now turned bitter. He started attacking me over every minor mishap, making me lose the power to think straight without criticizing myself. He attempted to cripple my brain by comparing me to his exes. He knew how bad of a fury it could send in a person, but his initial plan was to turn me into someone insane. He barely took time for me as communication between us became no less than a struggle. When I desperately wanted to reach out to him on certain days, he avoided me, indicating that my presence did not matter to him. Yet, I never understood his hidden agenda or the things he was hinting at. I never understood why he tried to steal my individuality when I always treated him as my counterpart. He may have had a bunch of women around him, but at this point, my concern was not a mere affair or his cheating nature since I could not mold him into a new person. But I had to assert my individuality if I wanted us to coexist as equal beings.

Time was slipping quickly from my hand, and I still had no idea where we went wrong. I could see the visible annoyance in his nature, but before I could comprehend his changing attitude, our relationship shifted toward a dark abyss, coercing me to accept behaviors that contradicted my values. All my life, I had lived among people who backstabbed me, but when he entered my life, I never considered him to be the destruction of me, so how could I have accepted the reality when he was my last thread of hope that I was holding onto?

I remember how I was left to deal with emotional trauma when he did not feel a thing. I felt the heavy weight of depression settle upon me while he stayed with his women. Everything was right before my eyes, yet I refused to believe he could betray me. I could have cried and fought, but what was the end of that? I had no other way out than to accept the feelings of unlovability and resort to isolation. He made me a prisoner of a narrative that portrayed me as the problem. People who knew me never mentioned this to my face, but I could tell from their eyes that they pitied me for ruining a man as gentle as him; what a lie! But these passersby were never my offenders, for his cunningness fooled them.

He was a man with subtle manipulations like a slow poison, and I found myself believing in a narrative that belittled me at every turn. He purposely compared me to others, imposing the idea that a person like me was not good enough for him. I, in turn, fought desperately to defend my character, but to what extent could I maintain my composure? His words woke the long-slumbered rage within me and fueled it until it finally became capable of burning everything to ashes. However, where the rage had its place, it remained a hidden truth that his words broke me into bits. I never allowed any of my emotions to be unveiled openly; I knew he would benefit from my vulnerability, but the constant comparison with his exes made me unleash the fury.

This remained my biggest regret when I allowed him to sneak peek into my vulnerability. To tell you the truth, I was not inherently weak, but love had perforated so many holes within me that now I wanted to crawl back to my den and hide from the cruelty of those who used the weakness of their loved ones against any backdrop and as much as my heart exploded to when I learned about the truth, this was the reality—the guy I loved so dearly was the person who would never shy away from abandoning me.

He had conditioned me to isolate myself away from my family or friends and dared to trigger me when I shrank my circle so that I could dedicate my entire world to his existence. Even then, his every action intended to humiliate me. His behavior toward me added resentment to my life, threatening to consume my once-happy household. Yet, I felt powerless to break free from the restrictions he had imposed on my life.

The truth was, isolation became my reality, and for the second time, I was about to commit the same mistake of confining myself between the four walls because love blinded me. His control extended to my very movements. He was a puppet master pulling the strings of my existence, and I was dancing to his beats. How foolish do I have to be to make this man the lead of my life while he loathed to take accountability for the steps he took? He loved blaming me, yelling at me, and hurting me, but he could not own up to his actions. Even when I had a series of evidence—the undeniable ones you see, he brushed them off as if he owed an answer to nobody.

I recall how his actions made me alienate myself from the world. His fear turned me into someone who refused to hang out with her close ones since he always found a way to use it against me. I do not know how it was always my mistake, but he knew how to use my life against me. I realized living my life was a form of punishment that he used to his advantage. He apprehended me with the handcuffs of exploitation while he lived his best life outside of our sphere. I was scared of him cheating on me; I feared him hurting me, and so the once vibrant person I knew myself to be was slowly replaced by a version molded by his manipulation and coercion.

As time passed, I felt more and more stuck in the mire of depression. My desperation reached a tipping point, and I began worrying about the well-being of my children, who did nothing to encounter such a harsh reality of life. Desperate to escape this suffocating reality, I decided to uproot myself once more and move to a different state. It was the last ditch where, on the one hand, I wanted to run far away so that he could never find me, but on the other hand, it was a test of whether distance could mend our relationship. The decision was difficult, but I had to protect my children. I did not want them to grow up looking at their mother popping pills for depression. I knew his companionship was toxic for my heart, and I had to maintain the distance before I turned hysterical. The weight of my sadness indeed left me in tears and seclusion, but was there a better way to shelter my children?

The realization came a little late that I could no longer endure the oppressive weight of this relationship, but I still had a family to protect. Even though I met my destruction, I had to hide the wreckage of my unshared sentiments in my heart while pretending that nothing went wrong for the sake of my children. It was a courageous moment when I took the bold step and decided to confront the darkness, hoping that happiness lay beyond the sea of this toxic connection.

Even when I moved to another state, his manipulation clawed over my mind, leaving a space for doubt that perhaps a problem lay within me. His words resonated in my brain whenever I set the table—this is not how one sets the table. His memories frightened me, and his utterances that followed me to a different state haunted my new house. But not a thing changed in his life. He was still a woman's man, and I was a person waiting for his return even though I was the one who ran away from his sight.

A little while into my new house, as I began to settle down, he became a frequent visitor again, just as my heart desired. Yet, not a single thing changed in his behavior. He was still a manipulator who interfered a lot more now in my household. I was growing nonchalant about his attitude; maybe life snatched my power to feel a thing, or I was getting immune to his not-so-normal attitude, but I started accepting his arrogance. His distorted perception was now an everyday tale for me until a friend who, back in the days, tried to tattle over me decided to awaken me. God knows why I allowed this friend to enter my house even though she was more than capable of backstabbing me. However, for some reason, we connected for the second time, and the first thing she did was show me the reality. I remember how unappreciative I was for the mirror she showed me, becoming all defensive. I justified my position as I shared the accounts of the old days when we lived a perfect life prior to relocating, but somewhere, I knew it was a failed attempt to cover up the hollowness I was carrying.

Besides that, I had to free myself from his strategically planned life, where I was infantilized to reduce my thinking capability to a child. It still makes me laugh how I, as a full-fledged grownup, was subjected to a victim of infantilized treatment, where my ex-husband forced me to rely on him entirely, and when I trusted myself with him, he showed me his real side. I knew if I did not take a stand at this very moment, history would repeat itself, and I could not let myself make the same mistake repeatedly. I needed freedom to restore my individuality; I had to be my own person so my children could be proud of me.

Despite my countless attempts, my efforts were never up to the mark. I had to work tirelessly to meet his unreachable standards, yet I was never good enough. He made me feel shallow and showed his discontent with my presence. He considered himself a winning trophy that everybody would try to get their hands on, and I was among many who had to work hard even to come closer to his standards. Keeping his narcissism on one side, he had the knack of projecting himself as the package way out of my league, and I, on the contrary, did attempt to receive his validations. I believed every word that he uttered and allowed him to judge my appearance from his distorted vision, where he found every other girl beautiful but me. He dodged my calls on the weekend and mysteriously vanished from my life, only to return during the working days. His constant disappearance left me with nothing but questions that found answers nowhere. I was not a kid; I knew what he was doing behind my back, but my poor heart was already suffering, and no cure would ease my pain.

The weekends were cruel as he would block me out and turn off his phone, intending to indulge in unknown activities. He manipulated my efforts to keep him close and pretended he had never vanished. I was tired—tired of this constant push and pull where I had no surety whether he was alive or had deserted me to go to another land. I cried throughout the weekends, not knowing how to regulate my emotions normally. My heart sank as I tried contacting him, but he never cared about my feelings. This was his weekly ritual, but it took a toll on my self-worth, which was now completely worn out.

While I cried and yelled at myself, I realized I was no more the old me; instead, a dejected soul took over me. She had a dark aura that resonated with mysterious vibes, but when did I turn out to be spooky? I was scared of the person I was becoming. I feared for my children, who were victims of the consequences of my actions. They did not deserve to see their mother turning into an unrecognizable being. But nothing was in my hand; my heart found respite nowhere, and I wandered like a half-mad person searching for happiness everywhere. My boyfriend claimed his disappearance was a brief hiatus from his so-called distressing life, but what about my heart that knew what filth he was getting into while lost in his world?

The impact of his manipulation was stronger than one could predict. Without much effort, he made me feel inferior, as if everyone was better than me and I no longer belonged to the human race. There were days when I could not converse with ordinary people since they overwhelmed me. Even returning to my hometown was a relentless torment. My family could decipher the cues of my troubled love life, especially when he would purposely turn a simple conversation into an argument, emphasizing the fact that he was the boss of me.

I remember how much I cursed myself in a closed room; what did I do to deserve this fate? With every passing day, my mental as well as physical state was weakened. I questioned my sanity and guilt, wondering if others had been right all along. Were their warnings about my naivety and foolishness justified?

Chapter 9

"Own family is supposed to be your haven, no longer your battleground."

- Anonymous

My house, which was full of laughter in its backdrop, was now burning. Every passerby who crossed my house thought it was glowing, but only I could tell that this one person deliberately tried turning it into ashes. I still regret the day I considered him my companion. Lost in childhood memories, I thought betrayal was out of the question between us, at least since he was the person who met me when I was still a child. However, that day, I learned a harsh lesson: life was not as simple as it appeared from a distance. This man who once claimed to be my survivor was a torment for my family. He was the sort of man who loosened his grip on me when I most needed him.

My worst nightmare began when I heard the news of my cousin passing away. Apparently, it was just another departure of a kind soul from this world, but ask me whose world was turned upside down upon hearing the loss of this young man. He played a role that went beyond being just a cousin to me. His shoulder was there for me when I had no one else to rely on. He listened to my hurt and never judged me for all that had gone wrong. He was the truest friend, brother, and soul encompassing the tale of my aches.

His sudden departure from the world made my world fall apart. I wondered *how could this happen?* The worst part was my then-boyfriend refused to be the support I was yearning for. He could see me in pain, but he never had the time or the mental capacity to provide me with emotional stability, or perhaps he never cared about me. My self-centered boyfriend prioritized his routine parties over my grief. It was indeed the cruel twist of fate that stole away someone so dear to me, and all I knew was to weep and curse my destiny. On the stormy nights when darkness weakened my vigor, I wanted to rely on the man who should have been my highs and lows. Yet, my search for peace only revealed emptiness. The one I expected to stand beside me in the face of loss had vanished, and here I was, standing alone in the sea of despair.

The day my cousin departed this world was indeed a black day covered in sorrow where I was constantly getting melancholic flashbacks of his youthfulness. I received the news at the crack of dawn and was caught in disbelief. Life cannot be this merciless! I screamed, as my heart was pounding with dread. How would I survive without this man? In my grief-stricken daze, I stumbled through the morning. I felt scared and haunted by my self-made concerns; what if I never got to say my last farewell to my childhood buddy? I waited anxiously for my passport, hoping for one last chance to see him, but the uncertainty consumed me. However, I believe the universe decided to go a little easy on me this time. The same morning, a letter from the passport services department arrived, announcing a document I had long given up hope on—my passport. I finally felt that destiny granted me the means to bridge the physical distance between my cousin and me. It was as if the universe had answered one of my prayers.

Feeling broken and hurt, I hastily booked a flight. During those days, I met utter hopelessness as the airplane's engine hummed dramatically. At this point in my life, my boyfriend remained non-existent. Even though he was beside me, he never comforted me for a second. His comfort and peace of mind mattered, and he was unwilling to rot with me.

Upon reaching my hometown, I stood amidst the mourners at the funeral, and the world around me seemed to be blurred. No matter where I looked, it was jinxed by sorrow, but my boyfriend was not human enough to sympathize with any of us. My soul felt numb as I struggled to comprehend the finality of the moment. The earth swallowing my beloved cousin was too much for my wretched heart to take. How could I ever recover from this loss?

Returning from the funeral, I felt like a half-spirited person haunting my existence. I was falling deeper into depression, knowing nothing could ever fill this void left by my cousin's departure. The unexpected death of this young soul pushed me into the abyss of solitude, and there was no way for me to pull myself out. While I struggled with my pain, my boyfriend vanished into thin air, enjoying the beauty of life. He left his grieving partner to meet his parents, enjoy his nightlife, and catch up with his friends, but life was not the same for me. I had the responsibility of two daughters, and even when I was submerged in pain, I had to keep myself sane for the sake of my family. Isn't that what a responsible person should have done? I was already dealing with enough; on top of that, my boyfriend's nonchalant attitude was adding an uninvited layer of stress to my already destructed state. I questioned God why Lou had to leave. Why does He call good people this early? My heart felt torn between my sinking relationship and my cousin's departure, yet my boyfriend had his priorities set. Despite sharing the same household, he was distant from me. God knew where he stayed, but he did not return to the house for days and always kept his phone turned off when he was out—an apparent attempt to avoid getting in touch with me. Alone at home, I waited for his safe return and, at the same time, fought against my agony.

While I mourned between the grievers, my boyfriend enjoyed his time across the country, strolling on the beaches and whatnot. At this point in my life, when I look back and think about his behavior, I cannot understand how less of a human he had to be to mock someone's pain.

As we returned to the United States, we both were on the same flight, yet he treated me as a complete stranger and feared that I would attempt to share my pain with him. The hypocrisy struck me as he later rode back to our shared home in my car. What an unmanly demeanor he had! His inhuman traits utterly disgusted me as I came closer to the realization that he once again pushed me into a mess.

The loss of my cousin's death pushed me to the brink of depression, and my boyfriend did not allow me to recover from this pain. He did not have enough patience to let me grieve in peace. I questioned God while I cried: How could the person I loved so much turn into someone I didn't want to see? My heart was once filled with his love, but I loathed his existence now, and I felt disgusted standing with him under the same shed. At that moment, he was not a source of ease; he was the reason that added grief to my already tragic story.

I survived with no companion, none to rely on for the two long years. I refrained from complaining to anyone. It was becoming challenging for me to juggle between the responsibilities of maintaining a household and caring for my daughters. Every day, I struggled internally, and every day, I pretended as if nothing ever happened to me. Nobody knew how I bawled on those restless nights or why I had puffy eyes. His perpetual absence from the household created uneasiness in my heart, but what about when he stayed with me? Was there ever a good time between us when he felt I was his destiny?

I remember how much he hated spending time with us, and whenever he decided to be the stay-at-home dad for the day, he made me feel less than a woman and dismissed the validity of my grief. Attempting to avoid my grief-stricken state, he stooped to a level where he started dehumanizing me. He began mortifying me for sobbing over the departed soul, and his shallowness reached a point where he began suspecting my tears for my cousin.

In the heated moment, I argued with him, intending to prove the authenticity of my emotions, but for him, my tears were no less than a pretense. Angered by his words, I ended up uttering some harsh words for his family; however, what happened next was not something that I was expecting as his long-term girlfriend. This individual, in a moment of heated confrontation, crossed a line and attempted to assault me physically. The moment he raised his hand on me, I felt my blood surge to my head. It was a wake-up call!

In the name of love, I had tolerated every unjust treatment, but abuse was beyond question. I could not let my daughters grow up in an environment where toxicity is a frequent visitor. Throughout the night, I kept repeating the same scenario: I was not angry at his behavior; I was not furious; it was just plain sadness that took over me. He was a cheater and a liar, and now he turned into an abuser. What else was there to see? The irony lay in his hypocrisy; he could not bear a word for his family, but they could freely insult me. Why did he never take a stand for me when his mother verbally abused me?

Throughout the night, my mind fought the battle with my heart; both were equally hurt. The next day, I rushed to the emergency room, realizing that my physical symptoms hinted at a heart attack. As the medical professionals worked to rule out severe health issues, I tried battling with the belief that my depression and stress were the reasons behind my sickness. I was alone, tired, and exhausted, but I had to fight my way out of this depressive state for the sake of my children. I hated the fact that I was no longer the same person. My mental capacity did not allow me to share my love with them. I knew I was going insane every passing day, and I wanted to find an escape from the tight grip of depression and anxiety. I wanted to prove to them that their mother was still the same. I wanted to tell them that I could still find their comfort perron in me, but to do so, I first had to heal not for myself but for my children, who deserved to grow up in a safe household.

I stood my ground and stuck with my decision after the physical altercation. I demanded his disruptive presence to leave and declared that I no longer needed a good-for-nothing roommate. But the bitter truth was, somewhere, he had already planned to return to New York, and what left me broken was the fact that he had never intended to share any of this with me. Instead, he created this whole situation about him and put our already strained relationship at stake just so that he could return to his hometown, yet he was not man enough to say this to my face. He plotted everything, knowing he never had the intention to stay—what a coward, I must say!

As soon as he reached New York, the strain on our connection grew even more prominent. Reaching out to him was almost impossible, and his constant absence from the scene made it hard to trust him. I knew he was most likely to cheat now that he no longer had any strings attached to my house, and you see, women's intuitions have the power to decipher what was said behind closed doors. Not long after returning to New York, I discovered he was retracting his old ways. Once again, I was thrashed into my past, where my ex-husband cheated on me while he belittled my existence; however, this time, the challenges were worse, burdening me with stress that felt utterly unnecessary. While I was attempting to mend our broken relationship, he indulged with multiple women while I cried in a closed room. I knew my attempts were futile, yet I still held onto him.

Far from my hometown, he found his freedom in a multitude of women, but he thought I was naïve enough to never learn about his filthy acts. Nonetheless, I would call him rather naïve for thinking that he would never get caught that, too, in the era of the internet.

At certain times, I wondered why his mother never attempted to bring him back on the right track. She accused me of his wrongdoings, but now, when he moved to another location, was she happy knowing that he was no longer with me? To tell you the truth, his mother never liked me, and despite being together for fifteen years, I existed in her eyes merely as his friend.

Her unceasing interference in our lives was where my relationship started going downhill. She sent postcards and letters to her son, and at first, what felt like a genuine love of a mother for her son was later revealed to be a secret message, pushing him to sever ties with me. He remained blind to his faults and stayed hidden behind the maternal influence as if he were a toddler. She applauded his every wrong behavior and later on accused me of his actions. It was disappointing to see the lack of compassion from a fellow single mother. I had hoped for more empathy from her as a single mother, but she fell short. His mother's words assassinated my character. She called me names, and he stood there listening to her every word, at times agreeing with her.

His mother knew he would never shun her since she held his reins. She had the power to control him. It was ironic that he defended his mother from humiliation while he undermined my existence in front of my daughters. Her right to speak freely was upheld by granting her an easy pass, but what about me? He feared disrespecting his mother yet failed to see the disrespect I had to endure in the name of love.

My girls had enough of lying, cheating, and suffering before they became worn out, and I had to face harsh repercussions. One of my daughters moved out, and the other shifted upstairs.

Breaking my house into fragments is an act I can never forgive this man for. He knew how much I wanted to protect my children, yet he became the reason they had to push me closer to isolation.

He was also one big maniac whose absence extended to an unknown period, but whenever he returned to the town, he would wear the mask of the kindest soul you would have ever encountered.

I finally reached the point where I knew his toxic mind games had to be stopped. I needed to summon strength to break free from his toxicity. Going to church and seeking God's presence was instrumental in my healing. I wanted peace, and my search only ended when I began praying with a pure heart. It was during this time that I accomplished my first career milestone. However, my career growth was tainted by my boyfriend's mother, who believed that I would end our relationship once I became self-sufficient. However, let me be honest about her words. It was not the prophecy that drove my decision; it was the realization that fifteen years with someone who failed to uplift me internally was enough. I had to cut ties with him because he was toxic. I had to loosen my grip on him because he never gave me his name. I had to find an escape from him because he suffocated me. I was not leaving him because I now had money; instead, I was leaving him because I wanted to live happily.

Two years into my job, I decided to sell my house. It was a silent move, away from his view, but only I knew the amount of strength I had to put in to get closer to my emancipation. It was a necessary step since my granddaughter was about to be born, and I could not think of welcoming her into a house where toxicity had its influence on every wall. I refused to tolerate this man—I would no longer take his manipulation, lies, or infidelity. That was the promise that I made to me.

I figured it was my moment to stand on my own. I wanted to be free for my granddaughter; I wanted her to be proud of me. Even when she was still a fetus, she gave me strength I did not know I possessed. I sold my house and built another safe home for my children from scratch. The man who was the first least bothered with my decisions returned to my life during this phase. However, my doors were closed on him. I firmly refused to revisit what had been left behind—I did not want to recycle the rotten trash. The man I once considered my lover was jealous of my accomplishments. He could not comprehend how I managed to build a house, but I proudly showcased my ability to build a new life from the ground up. I had risen, and he could not fathom it. The years of deception and heartache had taken their toll, and I owed him nothing. But for some reason, he returned with the hope that I would be paying for nobody knows what damage. Where I should have sued him for mental damages, he brazenly asked me to write a cheque for me.

Generous me wrote him a $5,000 cheque that he claimed he was entitled to receive. This individual, a freeloader residing in my home, listed imaginary bills as though he was entitled to payment for replacing a lightbulb. In those moments, money did not matter to me. I had found peace after fighting with life for a long time now, and I could not let anyone destroy it.

Once he left, sleep came easier, and I knew now I could live my life with a clear conscience, knowing I had reclaimed fifteen years invested in what was nothing. Nevertheless, I was still satisfied, knowing his chapter was closed now. But someone as toxic as him would never be able to handle his ex-girlfriend's success. While I strived to improve myself, he squandered his life by gossiping and spreading rumors about me. He tried tarnishing my reputation and showed people how vulnerable I was. He tried to seek revenge on me, but truthfully, those who looked down on me were never truly mine. I learned this a little late in my life, but people who were constantly waiting for me to stumble taught me a hard lesson and trusted me; I would not have felt an ounce of hurt if it were not for the woman who birthed me. I was abandoned by my mother, sister, and everyone else who attended his wedding, leaving me to fight with my emotions and question why I deserved this treatment. I spent fifteen years devoted to him, only for him to marry someone he just met. His mother welcomed her but rejected me for fifteen years. Is there anything more unjust than this? I never understood why she despised my existence, but I believe it was God who rescued me from her wickedness.

Chapter 10

"Jealousy is a creator of demons."

- ***Wayne Gerard Trotman***

Every night that I slept next to him, I had to fight a war within me. Somewhere, I always knew he was not good for me, that he would be destructive for my being, but then I was madly in love with him. Every person who had ever loved could comprehend what it was like to avoid the negative energy that your partner radiated. Although it was too evident that he was no less than a termite in my house, I decided to blindfold myself for the sake of the fifteen years that I gave to this relationship.

I chose to devote myself to him, knowing that this man was more than capable of burning me in the flame of angst. While I slept and woke up next to him, I fought with my fear—with my pain in isolation since he had a life other than the woman he claimed to be in love with. I figured this later in my life, but he was the kind of man who would console a lady he met a few seconds back instead of hearing the pain of his long-term girlfriend. He was the man who was rarely emotionally available for me but had the best technique to offer for any woman who was consumed with woe. I could sense what games he had been playing. He had no patience left to tell with me, but when it came to the unfamiliar ladies—a thousand times!

My life found itself muddled after my cousin departed from this world. The sudden and unwanted news took me a long time to fathom the reality. I was devastated, and my existence found itself in fragments, but for my then-boyfriend, this was all a stretched drama that should have ended sooner than it took. He was no child but was pretty much aware of his actions; he had seen me hysterically sobbing as I sat on the cold floor next to our bed, yet he proudly chose to invalidate my feelings because the person who died had no connection with him. I begged him between my hiccups to let me grieve in peace, but he made a mockery of having basic human decency. Sometimes, I questioned God*: why did I meet someone like him? Why did I have to be entangled with a narcissistic beast?* But there was no answer to my pleas. I felt hopeless, and the emotional aftermath left me wobbling on the edge of a cliff. I wanted to fall down, but I had my children waiting for me.

Let me speak the truth: I was a non-vulnerable person; I had lived through the worst phase of my life, but nothing had stopped me from thriving until I met him. There was a time when I went through major conflicts with my ex-husband, and with zero financial stability, I was left on the streets with nothing but a divorce paper. Yet, even then, my spirit was not ripped in two. I still dared to stand up for myself, but the day I heard that my cousin, my only companion, was gone, I felt as if I was drowning in the sea of melancholy. But, for my boyfriend, it was a pretense that should be halted, for his comfort was at stake.

Still and all, I did not hound him for any attention; I just demanded a little more time to weep. I wanted to return to him as a normal person who had no sadness left inside me. I never thought requiring some time to heal would trigger him needlessly because if I put myself in his shoes, I could say this at the top of my lungs with all my honesty—I would have stayed beside him while giving him as much time as he needed. I could not bear to hurt the person I cared for, not even subconsciously. Nevertheless, this was all about the mechanics of love, and a handsome Lothario like him could never understand what having true sentiments was like.

Time moved forward, and I fought with the pain, all in isolation. I was already disappointed in my so-called potential partner and did not care about receiving any reliance from his end. Somewhere, I believed my pain had drastically increased because of his unbothered attitude. I wondered if he was even concerned, but nothing could be done at this point. He did not feel a thing when my tears fell on the ground, and trust me, he could not care less, even if I would have been found dead in my room.

In fairness, being ignored by the man you considered your world was the worst feeling I had ever experienced. I despised and loathed his existence, but I could not tell him that he was the demon haunting my household; I did not repeat these words to myself either.

As a child, my mother always emphasized the significance of a peaceful household, and similarly, I grew up in a household where entertaining the devil was taboo. It was a known fact among us children that letting the negative energy seep into us was equivalent to giving an easy pass to the evil spirit, and during those days when I was living with my boyfriend, I learned that it was what I was doing to myself, letting my boyfriend be the destruction of my peace. I was too blinded to discern what evilness was prevailing around me, and the day I learned about it, I was greatly consumed by his negative energy.

Not a single day passed when my boyfriend and I did not end up in a fight. However, every time we broke into a fight, I was labeled as a psychotic person. Even his mother, who lived miles and miles apart or, to be precise, in another country, always had unsolicited opinions to share on my mental health because his son had undermined basic interpersonal functioning.

You must wonder how she learned about our fights when living in a separate country. Well, her well-domesticated son had to darn every tiny detail about our relationship into his mother's heart without considering that he was invading his partner's privacy. For some reason, his mother never held her son accountable for our sinking relationship. But she always successfully managed ways to find faults in me. She was the typical old dame who never tried to accept me as her son's lover. She hated me to the extent that she wanted to get rid of me from his life, and for that, she was more than willing to take any measures.

I was not a kid who could not sense her hatred, but initially, I believed I would be able to make a home in her heart over time—I was wrong. I could have only made her love me if the foundation of her hatred was any stronger, but her disgust was baseless, so I thought I should learn to co-exist with it because, after all, I was in love with this man; I had to make some effort. Nonetheless, all my attempts were futile because the hatred was no longer restricted to his mother, but now he shared the same sentiments with her. I was sacrificing my peace, the sanity that I held dear to me, for a person who despised me.

I made a fool out of myself when I trusted this man as I slept next to him and allowed him to enter my house, not knowing that he wanted to pose a danger to me. As time went by, I began experiencing a weird sensation. I had to fight the battle to put myself into the slumber land. In the midst of pain and betrayal, I was left to deal with a new fear. The only time where I got the chance to come across peace was snatched away from me, and I had to clash against it in the darkest hour of night just to protect myself from the demon I encountered while sleeping; it was plain brutal, I must say.

I remember I stayed restless and paranoid, thinking something might go wrong. But I never knew what it was about; I only had the idea that my vague feeling was not something that should be forsaken. I might not have an answer to this creepy situation, but I desperately waited for the day when my feelings would not be negated.

Anyhow, I slept with my hands clenched tightly while my heart was in a state of perturbation. I thought my situation was temporary and I would soon grow out of this phase; however, I was again proven wrong. Each night's disturbance soon began taking the shape of an evil force trying to take me into its embrace. I had no idea what it was, but I could feel the presence of something—something unknown sitting beside me. The creature was not visible to my naked eye, but I could still feel the presence of something in my room, and that certainly was not my boyfriend. Initially, I did call myself paranoid, but as time progressed, it became too difficult to confront the unknown disguised in eeriness.

My nights no more offered me serenity. I feared closing my eyes; I feared blinking, for God knew what would be standing in front of me if I rested my eyes even for a split second. My mind was haunted by a series of questions that had no answers. I constantly asked why and how I was struggling; what was my sin?

Sleep also abandoned me on most nights, and when it did visit, it brought with it a parade of night terrors. All the sleepless nights were making me vulnerable as I hesitated to close my eyes and feared what would be waiting for me in the dark. My struggle was becoming worse, and I began experiencing frequent episodes of sleep paralysis. I still have the memory of those dreading nights when I felt my bed slightly sinking as if someone was attempting to sit beside me. Every time this happened, I woke up scared and trembled like a leaf.

Those were some silent assaults that I could share with none. How could I tell people that there was a presence in my room that could never be perceived from human eyes? Would they even hear me? My boyfriend already wanted to label me as an insane person, and telling him about this unusual experience would only give him surety that I had lost it completely.

Besides that, my children could never learn what was happening with their mother. I did not want them to see me in a weakened state. So, whenever I felt a presence in my room and an unseen power settling on my bed, my subconscious mind would wake me up instantly. During this time, my eyes always caught glimpses of the clock whose hands would freeze at 3:15 A.M. It was a reminder that a force that stayed powerless during the day engulfed me at night. Every time I felt someone near me, my fear intensified, and I looked everywhere to find a place where I could lean on, even momentarily.

Night after night, I feared falling into their trap and wondering what I did so wrong to receive His divine punishment. While I prayed and begged God to find an answer, I found peace as I grasped the Bible tightly. Its pages proved to be my shield against the fears that haunted my sleep. Whenever I observed a mysterious figure around me, especially in the darkness, the Bible held a grip on me. In those moments, I diverted myself to God. I wanted His and only His hand on my head. When the absence of light put restlessness in me, the Bible became my shield.

But I needed external protection, yet sharing a bed with someone who claimed to love me was worthless. Instead, his every action made me grow suspicious of him. I felt that his presence seemed to invite devil forces even more. I was defenseless and weak. I needed someone who could lend me his shoulder whenever fear would grip my heart, and I was sure that person could never be my then-boyfriend. He was a psychopath who lacked basic empathy!

I had to live through the nights when an invisible force seemed to assail me. Without breaking my sleep, I could sense that a being beyond my comprehension was ready to attack me. In those moments, the maximum my boyfriend did was to wake me up because how dare I disturb him from his precious sleep? I hated him; I hated his every act, but it was a paradox—I longed for his support, yet resented him for my condition. Somewhere, I was convinced that he was the reason behind these occurrences. I was scared of everything; even my shadow did not provide comfort. It reminded me of the nightmare that cursed my nights.

I stayed awake the whole night, and my mind remained conscious even when I slept briefly. I had no idea why the haven was punishing me like this, but it was making my heart a lot heavier.

Obligations followed my restless nights, be it school or work. I had to stay focused for the sake of my career, but my mind remained on edge. I tiptoed on the crag of sleep while I was afraid of stepping into the abyss of demonic attacks. My sleep paralysis continued and, in fact, became worse the same year, and what was restricted to the late hours of the night was now ready to be unfolded. The second episode of my sleep paralysis was even more unsettling than the last, but it opened the door of comprehension for me. This day, I recognized that this was no mere physical assault but a spiritual battle. A mere spirit was not haunting me; it was all planned by someone near me to turn me into a psychopath. I questioned myself: who could hate me enough to inflict pain on me? The answer was clear—someone who could not bear to see me happy. I sensed that the root of these torments reached beyond the physical pain; it was a matter concerning sorcery, and I was a victim of this act. All the clues hinted at his mother's involvement in some dark practices. Oh God, tell me this lady could not stoop this low!

These sudden attacks continued to surprise me from time to time. I found myself yearning to lead a life where I could sleep in peace. I did not want my children to learn about my condition; I tried to keep it a secret from them, so the next time when I felt the attack, I ensured that my babies did not hear a thing. On that day, for some reason, I chose to sleep on the bottom level while my children were on the second floor; even though I was scared in the darkness, I felt glad that nobody heard my screams besides my dog, who spent the rest of the night consoling me. Night after night, I battled forces that seemed to target me alone, forcing me to surrender or accept my fate, but the situation never made sense. Why was I suddenly targeted by something I had no business with?

From where I belong, you would hear people commonly uttering that appearances are often deceiving and the mask of godliness could hide sinister intentions. It was all the truth because my then-boyfriend was equally guilty of this trap. As I tried wrapping my head around the situation, I decided I had to free myself from his torture. I knew I needed to sever ties with his darkness and had to bring back my faith. I was in no state to understand his or his mother's situation. I wanted him to be out of my place this instant, but how would I explain to him that I knew the little games they were playing with me?

My last sleep paralysis was another unordinary tale that happened during broad daylight, around ten in the morning. I still remember how the morning sun flooded my room, eliminating all my suspicions that darkness seemed to blur into a baseless thought. In the clarity of daylight, I lay paralyzed on my bed as my eyes fixated on the handles of my dresser. It was that moment when a weird feeling crept over me. I could not be sure enough; someone was indeed there. I turned around gradually to see who it could be, and what my eyes saw next was the most dreading experience of my life.

To my right, there stayed a figure resembling my departed cousin. He was in relatively close proximity to me, lying on the bed. *How was that even possible?* My cousin was dead; this could never be him, but then, who was he? A sinful soul who wanted to harm me under the pretense of my cousin? This was evil—a pure satanic act that only my then-boyfriend's mother could have attempted. Apart from her, none was this heartless; even her son was a better human when he stood next to her. So many questions jumbled in my head in a split second, yet my body remained motionless. I could feel the invisible presence grasping me, but I lacked the power to free myself from it. I could not tell you how helpless I felt.

At that moment, as the piercing sun's rays broke me from subconsciousness, I saw the Bible a few inches away from me. It was kept right there on the nightstand, but I could not seem to reach it. The struggle between light and darkness lay in front of me while I was locked in my room, but I had faith that I would reach it, no matter how hard this satanic power tried to take me into its embrace. My fingers desperately tried to get the Bible, and the second I touched it, I could feel the visible change in his strength. He was getting weaker and weaker, and the grip was no longer suffocating me. Attempting to gasp for air, I rose and ran away from my bed. Everything was clear—I could not confront this any longer. The fear, the sleepless nights—everything was beyond normal, and I, as a human, did not stand a chance against it.

However, it was distressing to realize that the people I did so much for were the reason why I was stuck in this evil dupe. I remember the day when my boyfriend's mother hinted that I was trying to snatch her baby away from her. It was evident from her tone that she believed her grown son was threatened in my presence and that he did not want to stay with me; instead, he was living in captivity. I wondered how could a full-grown man who could cheat at any given time be kept in confines.

Fast forward to the day when I unexpectedly received a message from a psychic. Truth be told, if I had received those messages in normal circumstances, I would have marked them as spam, but with the condition I was dealing with, I wanted a ray of hope, and these psychics in their messages regulated the sentiments that I had long felt but struggled to articulate. I wanted to hear the words of assurance; I wanted to know that there were no issues with me since this man had only attempted to undermine my worth—I felt desperate for validation. He forecasted a lonely and miserable future for me, and I wanted to hear if that was my reality. I went to the psychic, and they gave me the reasons behind my plagued heart. They rhetorically asked me why I felt a burning rage for this man even when I claimed to be in love with him. It would have been a pleasure to share the same shed with him, so why did I detest myself from him? They questioned my love for him, making me ponder the reality. Their words tore me—pulled me apart, but they opened my eyes, making me believe that God had purposely sent them to me for this very reason.

My second encounter with a psychic was a little more detailed than the previous one. This time, they revealed that the evil spirit I was fighting with could have been a result of sheer jealousy. They further added that enviousness seemed to be having a significant hand in this matter. I shared my take on our conversation as I told them even though I was not famous, strangely enough, I, an ordinary person, was a target of insane hatred.

The psychic paused for a while before she drew the image of an older woman and a man engaging in dark rituals against me. Just one encounter with this person and my trust in my fifteen-year-old relationship turned into smoke. I grasped my heart, which was on the verge of sinking, and told the psychic to continue, as I still had the strength left in me. They further added that the culprit used pictures of me, my clothes, and my personal belongings to manipulate for black magic rituals, which meant it was done by someone who could easily access them. I knew it—I always knew who had plotted all this; still, on that day, my heart was bruised—I was betrayed by the man who was supposed to heal my scars. Here, I was left to deal with wretchedness when all I had was love for everyone. I never understood why I was backstabbed by my loved ones when I never did any wrong to them. Perhaps that was human nature; they always bite the hand they feed from.

Chapter 11

"In the end, you don't so much find yourself as you find someone who knows who you are."

- Robert Brault

How could I forget the days when I was consumed by nothing but darkness? After crossing paths with those invisible beings, I realized my fight was no longer with the humans; now, I had a force stronger than me standing right in front of me, ready to be the end of me. I was left to fight them, but was that even possible when I could barely trace their existence? My hands shook with terror, and my body seemed to be controlled by discomfort. *Oh, what was I becoming? Was it the beginning of losing my sanity?* Somewhere, I knew I had to fight these people hiding behind the devils, but the truth was the power that they used to shield them and inflict pain on me was a lot more dangerous than one could have ever predicted. The truth was out in the open; I simply could not confront a mere individual. I was struck by the entities controlled by evil forces, and trust me when I say my then-boyfriend shared his soul with the devil—probably, this would also be an understatement.

However, my circumstances were different now. In the bygone days, I would have allowed the devil to feast on me, but I had long abandoned the old version of me who desired to be fed on love. I was a soon-to-be grandmother who only had one priority: safeguarding my grandchild. I had to stand up for myself and my family and take drastic measures, for I was no longer battling a single person but had a new life to look after. You would never understand how strong this one relationship can make you until you become a grandmother yourself, and that was the case with me. I was excited to welcome those little pure footsteps in my house, but before anything, I had to break free from the curse I received in exchange for falling in love with the wrong person.

Eventually, I felt trapped in this cycle. I thought I would never go back to the person I was. During those long nights when I feared the mere idea of sleeping, I sat on the cold floor and sobbed until my puffy eyes gave up, but since there was a life still incubating within my daughter, I promised myself that I would fight back, I would emerge with power. But through what means? On what door should I knock to break this wretched fate?

Who was the power who controlled each one of us? A little close scrutiny made me realize that my answer remained in my question. The mercy was his and not in the hands of some human whose only source of entertainment was to make people go through affliction. I turned to him and prayed until I was heard. I was earnest in my pleas as I began my search for the higher power. I knew that He would never let me go astray. He would hold my hand during times of desperation and provide me the strength to conquer this battle, for my heart was never intoxicated by impurity. Though I did feel shattered from within, obviously, to be tormented by someone I have spent more than a decade with was the worst form of mental torture. Yet, I stood there, firm, waiting for my prayers to be answered by the greatest of all. Every day, I passionately wished to receive the inner strength I had not recognized before. Indeed, after spending years with this guy who manipulated me into thinking I was good for nothing, I began doubting myself, yet the moment I figured he toyed with my brain, I gathered the courage and began picking up my fragments—I was determined to work on myself.

However, before I rove into the lands of destiny, I had to kill the vulnerable, frail me. I had to extricate myself from the prison of his sins, and this was only possible if I prioritized myself over his memories. My daughters, witnesses to my pain, depression, anger, and rage, had endured enough. They have seen him belittling me; they have encountered how their mother allowed a random man to walk all over her. I knew I was the culprit who corrupted their childhood, but I wanted to put an end to this misery.

In my heart, I acknowledged the harm I had unintentionally exposed my children to. I stole their childhood and made them live in a place where every day was filled with mortification and subjugation. Nonetheless, I wanted them to return to me again, knowing that I had struggled, but now I was capable of protecting my family. I begged God to be my aid; I asked him with sorrow in my heart to take my sleepless nights and grant me peace. I lay on the bed wondering if I really deserved what had happened to me in exchange for all the love I had showered people with. I regretted making him my world when I should have prioritized myself. I felt like penalizing myself for letting him ruin my family, but was I really at fault? As compassionate as I was, I wanted to abandon the softness of my heart and ruthlessly wanted to shatter his world. I wanted to see his doom!

However, the day this tiny life announced its arrival, I was suddenly turned into a different person. I no longer desired to avenge myself; I no longer wanted to see his pain; instead, my then-boyfriend became a distant memory for me. My heart was not inclined toward him anymore; I did not even care if he existed or was dead. You see how the birth of my grandchild filled the void inside me entirely. At this point, I cared for nothing but the commitment to shield this new life from the devils waiting to ingest my family's happiness. I knew I could do this; I could feel the vigor in me. I was already walking on the path of self-love; what was left now was to gather the lost pieces of my being and stick them back together.

In the depths of my soul, I could not bear the thought of my granddaughter being immersed in that toxic aura. I had to do everything possible to resist his negative energy's gravitational pull. I was desperate to protect the little baby from the darkness that had consumed me in moments of pain and neglect.

As her grandmother, I naturally wanted to build protective walls around my grandchild. Part of me wanted to create a heaven for her, but rationally speaking, these walls would have turned out futile if I were unwilling to change; I needed to eradicate his remnant. The only option I had was to sever the ties with this man, and by severing the relationship, I did not mean playing mind games like a teenager; I genuinely wanted him to vanish into thin air.

I guess I had come a long way and was finally beginning to forget him, owing to this little being who had taught me how to cherish the blessings around me. All I craved for her was an existence submerged with purity and angelic light, shining into every corner of our home and lives. I despised the mere idea of associating her fate with this man's negativity; I feared that he would contaminate her as he did to me. I did not care if he fell from the cliff or his parties became hell for him; I simply wanted him to disappear and never show his face. I had to stand firm because, in that crucial moment, I realized I needed to discover a love for myself. It was not a smooth journey to begin with; at times, I felt devoid of self-love. Yet, paradoxically, I found myself pouring more love into this unborn soul than I ever showed to myself. Strangely, I accepted this unfair treatment for a long time. I always thought love was selfless; perhaps that was why I never loved myself, and maybe that allowed this man to treat me like trash. But who should I hold accountable when I let him demoralize me? I never knew what my worth was, but now that I had decided to evolve, I set a new worth for me. I knew I was fighting for something precious—my peace, sanity, and essence were all a massive part of my battle.

Being a human with a kind heart, I have had my days when I felt like falling back into my old pattern. Maybe I got accustomed to his dehumanizing nature, but on certain days, I pondered if this was the misery or the days I had to withstand with this absent figure. I confronted the loneliness but resisted going back to the man who made me feel like I was nothing for fifteen long years. I constantly reminded myself that I had never felt more isolated, even in his company. The wise decision was to let the loneliness creep into me for once and all. Let this fear end on its own. I could fight with it rather than the feeling of not being enough. I would not return to him even if isolation made a home out of me; I would live—live without this man. I had to weigh and differentiate between Angel and Satan and decide what was best for me. Yes, my heart desired to melt in his presence, but I continued war against my inner demons.

I refused to surrender to the familiar yet poisonous energy that had long tried to kill me. Even when nights found me on my knees and tears streaming down my face, yet in that struggle, I discovered a strange serenity. I knew I was paying the price through the sorrow, but the tranquility of those nights was worth it. At last, I was reclaiming the lost part of me! I was ending a fifteen-year connection; to do so, I required strength that only God could have provided me.

I believe this tiny being was sent into my life as a means to brighten it when I sealed the cracks, refusing to let any sunshine enter my life. God knew I possessed the power; I just needed a gentle nudge, and he specifically had to send this cute little creature to look after me. The ironic part was where I was supposed to take this baby in my embrace; God conditioned her to surround me like a comforting blanket—every moment spent with her made me grateful to God. Her cries were not a nuance but a blessing, and the warmth of her gaze made me want to believe that I was deserving of love. This bundle of joy encouraged me to forget the past and move forward with what God had given me; it was enough to live if I eliminated that one person happily.

It took me a lot of courage to convince myself that the decision was correct. If not today, then some other day, but it was bound to happen. At first, losing a partner did take a toll on my energy and emotions. To tell you the truth, losing someone never feels right, and especially losing a person who was not only your partner for fifteen years but was also a childhood friend, it had to be a disaster. But in this struggle, I figured out my hidden blessings as well, and with each passing day, I discovered that staying away from his shadow was making me stronger and stronger.

As time passed, my connection with my then-boyfriend came to an end, or more like I restricted all the ways that came to me. As usual, he also vanished and changed his number so nobody could find his whereabouts. However, how long could he have fun disappearing when he had no one to locate him the way I did? Strangely, I learned that he had access to me, yet I was locked out. He might have thought this would add to my sufferings, but I knew these were nothing but mind games, a cunning plan to maintain control while leaving me hanging in between. The question remained the same: was I willing to fall into his trap, knowing how he threatened the peace of my family?

Searching for the answer, I thought, *oh, he deserved nothing from me—my hate, my love; he lost the right over everything!* That was my decision; I knew what direction I had to take to protect my peace. I would struggle all I could, but going back to him was not an option. My resistance to his evilness paid me off in a way that I no longer waited for his call; I did not care if he was living or on the verge of death. I was tired of the mental strain I had been living with; I wanted to break free from his golden cage and run in open fields. The happiness I sought everywhere was now just a step away. I hardened my heart and allowed his every memory to evacuate my brain. Believe me when I say that his absence provided me with comfort. The spiritual dreams, attacks, and heaviness left my side the day I declared I was no longer going to indulge myself with him. On that day, not only was he cast out of my life, but it was the end of fear and horror-struck nights.

Seven months away from him, and I could not be happier myself. However, those lonely, cold days coincided with the merciless COVID restriction. Those tough days allowed me to reflect on what I really wanted in my life. I survived alone in my home for days, learning to coexist with loneliness while the world was shutting down. With no other option, I was forced to face the challenge head-on. I could not care about the loneliness from the end of my partner, but what pained me was the abandonment I received from the blood relations I held dear.

For the seven long months, no calls, no check-ins. It was just me against my coping mechanism. However, I managed to find the silver lining; I decided how much I meant to whom. I did not allow myself to bend down just because I was alone in the storm—I was ready to take the plunge in the uncertainty. Surprisingly, I was untouched by the virus even when I started visiting work. I wondered if I was really left alone or if God chose to protect me from the people who were not loyal to me. Was not that what I asked in my prayers as well? I was alone, but at least I was true to myself. But there were days when I heard his sinister voices trying to hold me back. They haunted me, predicting a future where I would die alone in despair. I still remember his exact words, "You will never find somebody, you will always be alone, and nobody will want to be around you. And you will always be lonely, and you will die as a miserable woman." These few seemingly harmless words of his were enough to pierce my heart. They paralyzed my thinking capability for a while and left me with the trauma of ending up as a lonely woman. Yes,

I feared ending up dead in my house, but was I ready to trust another man? How ironic it was that he made me skeptical of the whole of humankind while cursing me forlornness as if he deserved any better.

But I prayed to God to take me out of the gaze of this Satan; I wanted to be free from the imprisonment of his words. I believed for a long time that I had built a cult of my suffering; I deserved to live now, that too without doubting myself. I should not fear happiness, and right when I prepared myself to receive what God had sent for me, an individual dropped from the heavens into my life to hold onto me. I had not met this man for months, but he made me want to give in. We talked daily for hours over the phone, and after a long time, I felt as if I was finally being heard. I was no longer an isolated mess; instead, he made me feel as if he understood the demons I battled within. He was the exact sort of person I searched everywhere. From cleanliness to living standards, we were both on the same page. I questioned God, could this man be trusted? Was he sent in an answer to my pleas?

Meeting this man was nothing like how I predicted it to be. I was hesitant at first, but then I realized he was easy to talk to and a kind, gentle person who I believed was on the journey of proving that not all men were like my ex-partners. Our deep conversations made me wonder if God had explicitly tailored him for me. He validated me and made sure to comprehend my past rather than make me believe I was the issue. He was an eye-opener that made me see the goodness in this world.

Talking to him was like encountering a mirrored version of myself; we shared the very essence of my quality of life. I was genuinely stunned by the similarity—he was certainly sent to share my agony. This person made me realize how wrong I was to judge all men from the same lens because of my past relationships. He showed me what an actual human was like. Even during hardship, when the world seemed to crumble, he gave me a reason to live. His existence was no less than a blessing for me; I recognized that my prayers had been answered finally. He was the exact kind of person I ever asked God for. He knew how to affirm me without making me believe that I was asking for too much. He became the antidote to the dismissive voices in my head. The bar was low before he entered my life, but he raised it and taught me how I should be treated.

Chapter 12

"Stab the body and it heals, but injure the heart and the wound lasts a lifetime."

- Mineko Iwasaki

In the beginning, I believed I was a mere human who had a bit of tough luck when it came to my romantic relationships, but as time passed, I began to realize not only my ex-husband and childhood friend whom I trusted betrayed me but also the people who shared blood with me turned out to be something else.

All my life, I had recurring nightmares where snakes were attacking me, yet I brushed my concerns, believing that I never wronged anyone, so who would want to hurt me? However, I failed to grasp that enemies are not precisely the ones who inflict pain, but enviousness plays a vital role when it comes to plaguing the rusted walls of the human heart. Unfortunately, for me, those snakes turned out to be my siblings and my mother—tell me, was it my fault that I trusted my blood relation? Not in my wildest dream could I have figured out that those dreams represented my family. What a doomed fate I was born with! And today, when I look back and think of at least one person who stayed with me, I find it hard to say that only darkness surrounded me. It was the bitter truth, but it was my reality; if I had to heal from it, I had to accept it. I had to accept the fact that my sister betrayed me—I had to live with the fact that my mother chose to believe a random man over me.

In the moments when I was struggling to the extent that even my shadow started annoying me, I struggled to understand why my loved ones backstabbed me. Every day, I woke up wondering about my crime that made everyone despise my existence; I never betrayed anyone, yet they formed an alliance against me, but for what reason? Was not it enough that my life tried to bring me down enough? I was surviving on no love; I was moving forward even when my legs gave up. Apparently, people believed I had been living a good life, but only I knew what it was like to live with scars that neither stopped bleeding nor their intensity became any lesser with time. During those days, I desperately yearned for someone to snatch the darkness away from me, but nobody was ready to hold a hand out. I tried to push it out, but it gripped me tightly. I tried running away toward the other side, but even their betrayal and painful memories were ready to consume me there.

Growing up, I realized my life was a little too bumpy compared to my siblings, but I never complained to God. I was the sort of pushover who never thought anybody could possess evilness; I always believed everybody had their reasons—that God made everything with goodness.

I regret having a soul like mine where I always strived to see the good in people, to believe in the inherent kindness of humanity while they threw rocks at me, not caring about the bruises they embedded in me. Yet, time and again, I have been proven wrong. If I talk about my family and this one person who I thought was supposed to lighten my world, I showered every ounce of my love on them, and what did I get in return? Emptiness! This man stole everything from me; he stole my family, my mother, and my siblings, who were supposed to stand with me because I was their blood, but they chose a guy like him over me. That was the irony of my life where a manipulative liar won over my family, and they, being the epitome of naivety, quickly trusted his every word as if they never knew me. I knew I was capable of fighting any battle, but the force that was conspiring against me was the people I had loved all my life, and this one truth was more than enough to tear me apart. When I saw the pictures of my sister hanging out with this man, I fell on the ground, baffled and taken aback by his evil plans.

The pain of heartbreak was no less than a physical death to me, and if I am honest, it stayed with me even to this day, constantly reminding me that I do not deserve to be loved. To tell you the truth, I somehow accepted this as an absolute reality until a tiny being entered my life, making me stand tall once again. Oh, the warmth I felt when I held her for the first time; I knew my life was going to be about her from this very moment. I could not care less how agonizing my tale was; I wanted her to see me as her companion, ready to bring happiness to her face and not as a gloomy person who had nothing to offer but pain. My granddaughter was a little bundle of joy for me; her little feet and small acts of naivety added light to my already dimmed life. She helped me understand that if I did not wish to escape this darkness, no one could help me break free from my reality. However, when could her little existence chase away the darkness that had encompassed me? Yet, she did show me a way—I could not let the unanswered questions plague my mind. I need to find a cure to this madness, knowing that betrayal did cut me deep; it left scars that may never fully heal.

I was deceived by those closest to me; they shattered my trust and broke me into pieces. They gave me a reason never to trust those who identify as humans; they were born to sling mud at each other, which also summed up my case. I was innocent; I was a victim, yet I was depicted as a villain. I never demanded anything from anyone, but the bare minimum they could have done was to trust me instead of believing the man who was the reason behind my destruction. I wondered why and when this man became such a significant part of my family that they prioritized him over me. My mother was cooking food for him out of nowhere, and my sister, who had never met him before, became his best buddy. It was funny to see the sudden change in their dynamics; this man was indeed significant in their life.

But was he ever an essential part, or was it just that my family would have prioritized anyone as far as that person was connected to me? I have searched for answers in the darkness; I have tried looking for an explanation for their act, hoping it would provide me with a bit of tranquility, but all my efforts turned out to be worthless when I realized I was knocking on the wrong door while searching for the answers. But even as I tried to make sense of the chaos using what little wit I had left in me, I was met with further betrayal.

After becoming a grandmother, I thought my mother and sister would be more accepting of me, but it was quite the contrary. My sister, who should have warmly hugged me upon my granddaughter's birth, chose to make my happiness turn sour because she felt like refuting me. If I ever get a chance to say this at the top of my lungs, I would never fear letting the world know that she was a liar and deceit was her companion. But what I feared was becoming like her; I feared that we shared the same blood, and what if I had the tendency to become as evil as her?

Even though she was my sister, she could not bear the sight of joy stepping the threshold of my house and always planned to become the termite for my family. I could have easily refuted it, but she was my sister! No matter how much pain she had inflicted, I could have never treated her in the same way.

During this time, when I had nowhere to return and no way to lessen my pain, I prayed to God. I questioned him and pleaded in front of Him. I shared my pain with Him; I told Him how the world has always been unfair to me. I wept until my hurt—until the physical pain took over the emotional hurt. I cried over the lost fifteen years because I had no one I could turn to and tell that I was in pain, but when I met God, I realized this was where I should find my answers. This was where I could reclaim my lost parts and become whole without looking for someone obliged to be my other half. I wanted to redeem myself from this sinful life of darkness; I wanted to become my own person like I used to be.

I was hung over the betrayal that I received from my family in different shapes because it was not just a betrayal from an outsider; it came from within, from my own flesh and blood. My sister joined forces with my ex-boyfriend and my former friend from whom I had long distanced myself. I would have allowed it to pass until it was no longer my business, but they chose to take their revenge on me by making me the talk of the town. And why the revenge when I should be the one ruining their lives the way they destroyed mine? They stabbed me in the back, and worse yet, I learned that my sister was the biggest support to my ex-boyfriend's multiple cheating plans. She was the one who lured him, introduced him to different partners, and encouraged him to cheat on me because God allowed envy to plague the heart of my sister.

However, I still do not find blaming her worthwhile. God could have never parted us if my ex-boyfriend had ever respected our relationship. This man not only betrayed me and cheated me but also snatched my family—my rock, my support system from me. On the days when I should be celebrating the birth of my granddaughter, I was drowning in sorrow and loneliness, abandoned by those I thought would stand by my side through thick and thin. Probably because I wanted to share my happiness with my family members, I felt the pain of losing my close ones more at this point in my life. I remember shedding tears through the sleepless nights while asking God why my family could not rejoice with me. Why did they always look for moments to drag me down further? My loved ones provided me with no respite; instead, they were the slow poison that was neither letting me live nor allowing me to die.

I remember how I tried to sustain the love in my heart. I remember how I was the only one who tried to bring the family close as I traveled miles to see glimpses of my mother and siblings. I was a mother figure to them; I practically looked after them in the place of my mother, but now, when they were grown-ups, this was how they decided to pay me back. I was such a fool to even think of bonding my children with their aunt. I thought it would be good for my children to grow up knowing the warmth of family, but maybe love was never meant for me. And here I was, sitting all alone, abandoned! Nonetheless, my tale was not only about the unfair sentence of abandonment that I received; what angered me was their obsession with throwing dirt at me while I did absolutely nothing to hurt them. I was angry because the picture they aimed to paint was a well-crafted story in which they remained the protagonist.

But as I said previously, I had to find courage alone. This was my journey, and I was responsible for whether I would sit here and cry or conquer the battlefield. Everyone might have been waiting to see me fall flat, but I was unwilling to lose this race. I won't fall into despair anymore; I have had enough of this sadness. I refused to let the darkness threaten me. Blocking out the memories, the pain, and the faces of those who had forsaken me, I decided to focus on what was good for me. It was not easy; the darkness was now a part of my soul, and getting rid of it was equivalent to taking out an organ without any sedation. There was no way I could tell how long it would take me to move past it, but I was glad at least I was ready to accept my present and to leave my past behind. My past might be threatening to drag me down, but I was ready to fly high as I still had a few constants in my life—my daughters, my granddaughter, and the happiness that they brought with their existence.

As I tried to forget my past, the grip of darkness loosened its hold on me. My scars were still there, but I no longer saw them as marks of shame. While I tried hard to maintain my relationship with my sister or then-boyfriend, it seemed like everyone around me was quick to point out my flaws, convincing me that I needed fixing. The betrayal may have shattered my world, but now I knew it was not me who had to fix myself; it was them who always made me feel as if I was not good enough for them. I was happy to realize that my self-doubt was becoming cloudy as I distanced myself from them, and I stopped questioning what was wrong with me; why could I not fit into their mold of perfection?

Before I made peace with the broken ties, I tried to understand them, intending to mend the relationship, but my attempts were met with accusations and cold shoulders. Even my sister, who was once my closest friend, turned her back on me, swayed by the manipulative words of this man. She thought I was accusing her of being with my ex-boyfriend, but I only demanded an answer because I wanted to protect her from this man's wickedness.

I could tell he was using my mother and my sister to instill his manipulative stories; his tricks were simple, yet my mother and sister were more than willing to be betrayed by him. Nevertheless, I could still not comprehend how the people I loved could so quickly accept his deceit over my loyalty, how they could abandon me in favor of someone who had caused me immeasurable pain. And this was not the end. There came the ultimate betrayal—they attended his wedding, celebrating the happiness of the man who had brought me nothing but anguish. They cared more about his happiness than mine, which was evident from their actions; I did not need any proof to support my claim.

I was a pure-hearted person who never doubted anyone's intention, but trust now was a luxury to me. I desired to trust none; I did not want to go through the same situation ever again. Soon, I learned the only place to put my trust would be at my Lord's door. He would not betray me; instead, He would become my savior. I returned to faith, not allowing the evilness to take over me. I vowed that I would not abandon my belief; I know goodness still exists in this world, even if I was unfortunate. I would continue to fight against the darkness; I would continue to see good in people. Regarding trust, I would always try to restore my faith in God's creation, but my wounds were still too fresh to take another blow.

Chapter 13

"A higher truth cannot be overthrown by a lower lie."

- ***Matshona Dhliwayo***

For as long as I can recall, I have never shared my agony with anyone but God. I pleaded with Him to show me the light at the end of the tunnel so that I could free myself from this misery. I did not care if it was the faint one; I wanted the hint of hope so that I would not lose this battle. I was exhausted from living as a murky shadow; it was as if my soul was drained.

Even when I was on the verge of giving up, I could gladly say that God did not give up on me. When the darkness consumed me, leaving me with nothing but a void, God sent this little being to my world, and I realized I still had a lot waiting for me ahead. I realized that God had descended my granddaughter from the sky into my arms so that I could allow the light to enter the cracks within me. Yet this was neither the end of my happiness nor the tribulation that was coming my way.

In fact, it was His way of providing me with the strength that I would require to fight the upcoming wars. While we had our celebrations, I started my search for something unknown. I had the urge to find the intangible at a place where I would no longer fear the intrusion of evil. It was not enough to laze in the happiness she brought; I needed more. I needed to dive deeper into the recesses of my soul and unearth the amass of inner contentment—that was the mission God had sent me.

People wounded me, and I have cried enough about their abandonment. I wanted to make myself strong enough so that I could renounce my sorrow and let the joy overpower my heart. I despised the idea of crying over the spilled milk—*so what if my loved ones betrayed me?* I was stronger than this. The pain was inflicted on me by those I loved, preaching to me that I had to live without their support; I knew I had to reclaim my happiness from within. But I was not sure where to find the search of what I had lost in the process.

Let me be honest: I knew I was looking to acquire something I had left in the bygone days. From time to time, I wondered if it would be possible for me to reclaim what was once mine. Where could I trace the long-lost sparkles of me? Oh, how could I forget? The old music that had encompassed nostalgia in it—I can always gain my missing pieces from them.

The second I found the antidote to my yearning for what I had lost, I turned to my old companions: painting, music, and driving alone. I began enjoying my slow life while humming my favorite music or, at times, simply looking at the sun setting, reminding me that there would be an end to my wretchedness. This was my time to live while having an insight into who I was as a person and trust me, I could not be happier to walk on the road of self-discovery. It was indeed challenging, and at times, I was scared of regression, especially falling back into my old pattern. But in the middle of overcoming my fears, I realized that the demons were not targeting me only—they were looking for more!

There were nights when I could not sleep a wink. I bawled my eyes out until my heart stopped bleeding. I found myself fighting the invisible demons, trying to possess my body and make me one of their own. But was I ready to give up? No matter how much I cried, I was not a weakling. Even if my legs gave up and I felt crippled, I was not ready to give in. And maybe—maybe God liked me for my strength, but I could tell he refused to let go of me. It was as if God himself decided to help me this time.

I never believed in angels' numbers, but this time, it was evident to me that God was sending angels to help me. I turned to unfamiliar places, but at every turn, I found my eyes on Angel's number. I could have concluded it as a mere coincidence, but any sane person could tell multiple instances could never be an accident. I knew what I was doing; it was the right path that should not be forsaken.

I remember driving for hours to escape anything that was haunting me or anything that was threatening to become my heartache. I did a series of assignments in a land far from my house just so that I could distract myself from the grip of my past.

So far, I lived a life rushing to reach a destination. God knew which destination, but when I stood there on the battlefield, I realized I never had any destination. While I lived my life for others, nobody sacrificed themselves for my peace. But who should be blamed for it was the self-imposed destruction?

But I certainly found clarity the day I began moving toward the road of divinity. Everything that caught my sight was symbolic of His kindness. He made me search for the courage to confront my pain and let the resentment go. But let me tell you, I did not choose the orthodox way to heal myself. I did not start my journey by soul-searching; I wanted to live my life while finding my true self. I made time for joy, and above all, I made time for accepting that I had needs. I began looking at myself like an ordinary human with yearnings and went to where I could find my missing pieces. I was no longer a super mom; I was me!

My plan was to become selfish—utter selfish so that I could put myself before anything. During those days, I visited shores, and road trips were my absolute ally. They comprehended the silence that my closest ones failed to decipher. They knew the meaning behind the unsaid. These were the places where I did not have to explain myself to anyone; these places did not burden me with any expectations—they only had peace to offer. The soft breeze and the leaves falling around me—the tides slowly reaching the land and sand where I could bury my apprehension was how I chose to bring peace to myself. I was growing into a better person and finding my lost self. I liked how I no longer felt like the victim but gradually became an ordinary human. I was a warrior, ready to fight anyone that would try to harm me and my family.

I was at that phase of my life where I was slowly forgetting the fear of people leaving my side. I was healing; I was in the middle of rejuvenating. I would not claim my healing was one hundred percent; I was still struggling with accepting that my goal in life was never to please anyone. It was a fight to become my true self. I was telling myself every day, *why should I care for people when they never cared about me?* Perhaps this was why my devils hated me. They realized I was leaving them behind, and they could not bear to see me rising. They knew I would stand firm; the person I was becoming was enough to ruin their generations. They had to break me before I became their demise, so they changed their strategy; they needed a better plan.

I was no longer their primary target. They stooped the lowest and started attacking those I held dear to my heart. They knew I was ready for anything, but I could not endure the separation between my children, and they made good use of my fear. They constantly desired to snatch what little strength I had gathered and to win their battle; they once again chose the road of evilness. What else would one expect from people like them who sinned by breaking a family?

For some reason, my urge to go back in time triggered them. They probably knew in the old times that nothing could withstand my positivity. They feared my power, and right when I was ready to build myself for the third time from the ashes, they sowed the seed that would crush me. Remember how much I was happy when my granddaughter was born? These people used my happiness against me as they tried entrapping my daughters while spreading malicious lies about me. But those were my daughters; they would not trust some baseless accusation from an outsider. I had faith in them. They grew up looking at me; they had witnessed my journey. Their personalities, even their appearance, were a reflection of me, so how could they doubt me? Yet again, I was at a loss. You ask what my crime was. I was trusting the wrong people.

I still wonder how my eldest daughter, for whom I had struggled so much, became a victim of their lies. I still do not have a plausible explanation that will provide respite to my heart. She was my flesh and blood; how could she believe the words of a complete stranger over mine? They say the firstborn is always the closest to the mother, and that was true in my case as well. She was the closest to me; we had struggled together, and I was the ultimate support system for her.

Our bond grew stronger when she gave birth to her child with an uncanny resemblance to herself. *After being a mother, she would discern what it took me to fulfill my duties,* I thought, but ironically, she also abandoned me when I needed her the most. I was the woman who had witnessed multiple storms, but each time, I came out strong enough to fight any unfortunate incident without any external force. Now, when my child was standing in front of me, I could not help but feel the intensity of my helplessness. How could I ever fight someone who grew up in my womb?

By the time I learned that my daughter had fallen into the trap of misunderstanding, it was too late. By then, she had cut ties with me, accusing me of a crime I never committed. Her tone and accusations pierced me deeper than I care to admit. I questioned God: *why would someone target me this way? All I ever wanted to do was live my life in peace. I distanced myself from the world so I could stay away from the filth. What did I do to receive this punishment?* I cried when it came to my understanding that my child was no longer mine. This was the child I incubated within me for nine months, the one who learned to walk holding my hand, and this was how I was being repaid for bringing a life to this world. I served her hot meals while struggling to provide her with a good lifestyle, and the same child decided to break our bond just because of a few rumors that found their way to her home. It never made sense to me how we were torn apart because of some baseless accusation. Was our relationship always this frail?

Witnessing a child's mind tainted by complete nonsense is something that can shatter a mother like nothing else. Weirdly, it was a secret for a very long time, but even when I learned about the reason behind our broken ties, she chose to seal her lips. Nevertheless, there was no point now when her hatred towards me was visible. She loathed me; she hated the sight of her mother. My reality was harsh, but it was the truth. I did not care about the authenticity of the news; all I knew was that my daughter took the burn for no apparent reason. She was frustrated and in pain. She might have lost the senses to differentiate between right and wrong, but her actions shook the foundation on which I was standing. She was desperate to push me away, and in doing so, she did not mind ending her relationship with the only sister she had.

All my life, I saw a dream of my daughters growing old together with love in their hearts. I wanted them to become inseparable so that no one could hurt them. I wanted them to set the example of unity while supporting each other through thick and thin. But I could have never predicted my firstborn would crush my dream this way. The devil, it seems, found his way into our lives once again, intending to bury me under the rubble of my dream. I could not explain what a tragedy it was to see my children separated, unwilling to look at each other. It broke—I accept that—it did!

My mind, being the ultimate enemy of mine, kept on playing the flashbacks of their childhood—the days when my firstborn took the responsibility of her youngest sister. How could I forget when I was the witness of their love? A sea of tears was inside me, turning into a torrent, ready to take over the world. I wanted to yell and cry, but would that have made any difference?

Today, when I look back, I feel disappointed in myself for letting dismay control my emotions. Why would I consider myself cursed when God had been there for me all along? I was the most fortunate child, and that was my vision growing up, yet after a few incidents, my love for God faded, and that was my crime. I could not let my trust wander; I could tell He was still standing with me during the darkest night.

I might have felt hopeless for a while, but I was never the person who forgot the kindness He had bestowed upon me. I knew He would test me in the areas I had committed to, but He would never test me beyond my strength—that was the greatness of the Lord. I had to return to Him, not only for the frequent visits but to devote my heart utterly free from all the grudges. I was glad I learned His secrets sooner and allowed the resentment in my heart to escape. To pave my path toward divinity, I forgave those who tried ruining me—who messed up with the institution of my family. I told myself forgiveness is a huge step toward healing. Let them go, but never forget what they did; never let them betray you for the second time, but at the same time, do not let their negativity consume you.

I might be in pain, but I decided to search for peace in the knowledge that my conscience is clear. I have loved my children, and every person who has ever encountered me on my journey is a witness to my love for them, and nothing can tarnish that love. I could never forget the betrayal—the accusation, but today and forever, I live with the hope that my truth will prevail one day.

Chapter 14

"One word can end a fight; One hug can start a friendship; One smile can bring Unity; One person can change your entire life!"

- ***Israelmore Ayivor***

All that happened in my life was no less than a haunting tale. The people who should have stood with me became the reason behind my apprehension; the people I held dear abandoned me on a desolate land, yet you look at my strength; I refused to let anything be the end of me. I rose from the ashes every time my loving family instigated a fire within me. I withstand all those scars that wounded my body. Indeed, I still had to meet my demise; I was still counting my breath, but to tell you the truth, something inside me died the day my daughter turned her face away from me. The thought of losing the one I brought to this world was enough to suffocate any mother, but you look at my misery; my nightmare became my reality.

My mother, my siblings, and now my daughter were under the influence of some stranger and his baseless rumors, and I had no say in it. I always wondered why his words had more power than my whole existence. *Why could not my family believe in me; why did a stranger's utterances hold so much significance?* But my sorrow lies in my helplessness, for I lost the courage to tell them my crime. Yes, it was my crime that I always loved people with whatever I had. I doted on my family; I selflessly gave my everything to them just to receive hatred and accusations from their end. The man I loved for fifteen long years—my so-called companion threw dirt at my character, and you know what was ironic? My family, who should have protected me in my absence, served as the fuel to burn my soul with the intensity that was lacking before. So why should I not refer to my love as a crime, for I received a heavy punishment in return?

In all honesty, they wanted me to become crippled, yet I still had the power to stand on my feet. They feared my strength; they knew I possessed the power to make them rue their very decision. Their fear led them to spit venom at my daughter; they used the last card they had rolled up in their sleeves, and I must credit them; it shook my foundation—be it momentarily. The loss of children, the pain of broken ties; oh, I have finally witnessed all that I feared, but hear me out, that was where they went wrong. They believed snatching the right from my daughter would throw me into an abyss, but they did not realize that they freed me from the only thing holding me back.

I was a loner; I stayed locked in my house with no human connection to vitality. I was at a point where I did not care for death finding my way; I was barely alive anyway. Especially during those long, isolated Covid times, when the world struggled to live together, I was caged in my room, wondering if I ever crossed my sibling's mind. Those were the days when I often yearned for a connection, a hand to pull me out of the depths of loneliness. It was an innocent, human urge to share th days of apprehension with a companion—someone who would lend an ear or listen to the things consuming me from inside.

I waited and waited for a mere gesture of concern; maybe dropping by was too much, but a call of reassurance once in a while would have hurt none. All I asked from my family was to remind me that if I died today, I had someone who would stand next to my casket, but the quietness of every passing day mocked my loneliness. Indeed, to die was no less than a nightmare for me! Covid was the time when people befriended their arch-nemesis, yet I realized I was unfortunate enough never to receive a message from my family, but did I weep over my wretched fate? Maybe certain times when my heart swelled with pain; however, the number of tears I shed was never my weakness.

I sobbed and yelled until my heart felt lighter, and the next morning, I returned to work as if the shadow of sorrow never touched me. I was unsure of how long I could have lived with my alter-ego, but I guess that was my way of coping with my agony. So what if I bawled until my eyes turned puffy? At least I did not beg anyone to lend a shoulder to me. Even when the feeling of forsake took over me, I locked myself in my house; I would never ask anyone to have mercy on me. Those were the days when the world was getting creepily silent, and only the screams of the viral infection were heard, piercing a hole within the walls of every neighborhood. I remember how scared I was thinking about the uncertain future. Nobody knew if we would survive another day; nobody cared about the long-lost days of broken ties, but even then, my family never cared about me. Even a pandemic did not raise empathy in their heart, and the long days of horror turned out to be a realization for me—Oh, my family never bothered to check up on me.

However, in the middle of the silence and isolation, right when I put my search for a companion to rest, I found a person unknown to me waiting for me on the far side. He was similar to everyone I met but was different on his own. He reflected me in his words but was not even close to who I became as a person. I wonder what mystery he held? Why did he choose to become a conundrum yet the answer to all my uncertainties? I never understood what he was in my not-so-magical world, but I concluded this man to be a person, seemingly sent by fate. He was ready to fill the void within me with meaningful conversations and genuine care—a perfect match for my dejected soul. Maybe God heard my pleas, or perhaps he loved my resilience, but I could not come up with a better explanation for the time of his arrival. His story was no different than mine; he was an isolated soul who was held captive by the loneliness of those difficult times.

Every now and then, I wondered why this man was sent to me during those months of solitude. I realized the power of prayers at that moment; I knew my pleas for a companion and tranquility paid off. Before this man entered my life, each day was a battle against the isolated figures haunting me inside my home. I struggled to break free from the ties that were binding me to my aches and were bruising me every day. However, through the quiet moments and deserted streets, this man made me see the spark that I had within me. This man told me I was looking at myself from the distorted lens of the world and that I should abandon the words people spewed to hurt me. He did not give me an identity; he did not impose his view over me; instead, he showed me a way through which I discovered my missing pieces. Each day, he pushed me closer to my liberation; each day, he provided me with the strength I had lost somewhere while battling against the devils.

I could not believe how this man, whose existence was hidden behind the screen, became such an essential part of my life in such a short time. Indeed, at times, I feared his goodness—what if he was the right hand of the devil? But honestly, my fear had nothing to do with his demeanor. He was a sorted man with nothing to offer but loyalty, yet I was not in the position to trust people, given that even my mother chose to betray me. However, he was the man who was sent in exchange for my prayers; how could anything go wrong with him? If I was precise, this man was not an ordinary person to me but someone who understood the depths of my struggles, someone who, despite having his brawl, was ready to stand beside me.

I could not trace the moments when he captured my soul, but gradually, talking to him became the only good part of my routine. In the moments of loneliness that used to haunt me once, I started to feel the presence of peace. During those days, the world may have been covered in darkness, but within the walls of my mind remained the image of a man who held a hand out for me, and I proclaim this today: I will never forget his kindness. He was the only person who ever tried crossing over for me; he went to every extent to ensure that I felt heard and cared for. He knew my heart yearned for a connection, and he figured out that even though I do not talk about my struggles much, I never received my fair share of love.

Probably, that was what I adored so much about this man—he did not need words to comprehend the state in which I was; he discerned my pain through the intervals behind the blank screen. He was willing to stand with me as long as I dared to let him inside my world, but was that even possible for a person like me whose heart was turned into fragments? And this mind of mine was no less than a curse. It never allowed me to forget my past. It mostly kept me entangled within itself. While this person stayed with me, I once again swayed over my thoughts, but I was not ready to give up on him, not this easily.

I still remember what it was like when I first started talking to him. His arrival felt like the beginning of a spring morning where the smell of flowers was becoming my reason to live. I was finally living a life that even I felt was too good to come true for me; I walked on eggshells, wondering when my life would turn upside down. Yet even while tiptoeing, I was happier knowing that he would hold me if I ever faltered. I could not question his kindness; he was a man who deserved nothing but love. This man changed me for the better, but somewhere, I still had the urge to share my happiness with my family, especially my sister.

At this point in my life, I had everything—a man who cared for me, peace, love, and whatnot- but God knew what else I was urging for, so I reached out to my family, who disclosed their true intentions. I could have never comprehended that my family was against my happiness; I was taken aback by their attitude toward the little joy that I found. For some reason, my heart always believed that my family was turned against me by my ex-boyfriend, but the day I allowed them to become the visitors of my happy dwelling, I realized they did not hate me because someone made them do so; they loathed me for my existence alone. They did not care about my happiness; they wanted to see me crawling and begging, and when they realized my days of sobbing had ended, they lost the last bit of sanity. The day I returned to my family, hoping to leave every disappointing tale behind, I learned how much they hated the idea of me living happily and freely for the first time in a long time.

I wonder if looking at me in pain ever ripped their heart? When I was about to give up on myself, did that make them curse the one who was causing my hurt?

My desire to share this joy grew rapidly; however, when I returned to them that day, I no longer craved their validation. It was to proclaim to the disbelievers that I had broken free from the chains they deemed unbreakable. For years, their skepticism had weighed me down, yet now, liberation was running through my veins—yes, I was alive once again. Those who always told me I could never leave a man like him behind, my victory was a slap on their faces. Look at me; here I was, living a life of happiness while leaving behind the man who threatened my liberty.

And I would not have won this race if it were not for the man who entered my life during the times of disaster. We had not yet met face-to-face, and we might never get the chance to look at each other in person anymore, but I respect his presence in my life, which challenged the essence of my being. He transformed my thoughts with each exchange and made me believe in myself. It was as if I had been reborn—as if the trauma of staying in that fifteen-year relationship had been taken far away from me.

It was not easy for me to leave behind a relationship as toxic as this, but I could not be prouder of myself for not letting his evilness consume me any longer. What was deemed to be my end—look how far I have left it, and it could not even find my traces. But the people I believed would become the equal companions in my happiness failed me once again. Yet, I still extended my heart to them; nonetheless, the responses that I received shattered me, reminding me that was how they have always been. Instead of celebration, I was met with condemnation.

The very individuals I hoped would rejoice in my liberation turned their backs on me. Their words were filled with empty promises of support; they stung with betrayal and deceit.

How delusional I was to spend years believing their assurances that they wanted to see me happy, but this time, their actions spoke volumes to the contrary. That day was another realization for me, and I learned that the love and loyalty I had invested in them were nothing more than a shattered illusion. My happiness was secondary in their eyes, but my ex-boyfriend's well-being was the priority. They prioritized the comfort of the man who held my mind captive for years.

The ultimate betrayal came when they not only renewed their ties with my former tormentor but actively participated in his marriage as well. He was allowed to live with another woman, but my mother and sister found it unfair that I even dared to think about my happiness. What a pity! And the worst part was yet to come. They attended his wedding to another woman; they fed him and cared for him while shunning me when I even tried to question my rights from them. In that moment, I saw my loved ones for who they truly were—complicit in my suffering, indifferent to my joy. It was painful to accept, but it was necessary for my growth.

I had to learn to find love within myself; I had to strive for peace, not from an external source—that was the agenda this man had taught me. I vowed to never again seek validation from those who had proven themselves unworthy of my trust. My happiness was mine regardless of what they thought. I had the right to love and be loved; I did not deserve to cry about the things I had no control over. This was my journey of freeing myself from anguish and heartbreak; I was enveloped in a juxtaposition of emotions, and I realized this uncertainty was justified; I was a human.

This time also served as a reminder that God never let my prayers go in vain. While I was skeptical of this man at first, I realized he was not even close to the men I had ever encountered. I questioned the purpose behind his presence in my life; I realized that perhaps he was sent to me as a messenger, a vessel for delivering the lessons I needed to learn, and somewhere I did believe I was not wrong. His insights and wisdom made me see who I was. He did not mold me as per his standards but pushed me forward to become my own person.

Through his influence, I began to see myself as an empowered woman. I did not fear disappointing people; I was unwilling to trade my peace for anyone's satisfaction. Ultimately, I conquered the darkness and rose stronger, becoming someone who could withstand any calamity. My life may have been quiet for now, but I often find myself reflecting on the days when my family, the bonds that shared the blood with me, betrayed me for a person they barely knew. There was a time when I felt stuck as if life was a stagnant pond that was shrinking and suffocating my physical growth and mental, emotional, and spiritual development.

No matter how much my life changes for the better, I will never forget this one person who entered my life during those dark times, intending to serve a purpose that was still hard for me to comprehend. He possessed a level of maturity far beyond my own and showed me a way to reexamine my thoughts. Though our paths have since diverged into two, I am forever grateful for his kindness and what he has done for me.

Regardless of my progress, I recognize that my journey is far from over. I carry the scars of my past experiences as reminders of the battles I have fought. But as I have always said, I refuse to let those scars define me. Instead, I wear them as my pride. Every person who has crossed my path and every experience I have endured has shaped me in some way, turning me into the person I am today. And while I may not yet be ready to start a new relationship, I am committed to healing from the inside and becoming the better version of myself. I still have nights when I find my heart restless, but then I find peace in my faith, knowing that a higher purpose is there guiding me. I am grateful for the strength bestowed upon me by the divine, which sustained me through my aches and sorrow. And as I look back on the person who once entered my life, I do so with gratitude and reverence, for he was indeed a blessing in disguise. He might not be aware of his impact on my life, but only I knew what nightmare I was living in before he crossed the threshold of my life.

Chapter 15

"When God is ready for you to move, He will make your situation uncomfortable."

- ***Germany Kent***

Is there anything left unsaid, or have I succeeded in pouring my heart out? I searched through my heart as I concluded the account of my aches. The day I thought of giving life to my fury was the day I decided to abandon the grudge growing inside my heart. I had enough of the hatred pushing me to return to darkness; I no longer desired to see them begging on my threshold. I was glad to observe the amount of peace God was sending my way, and I believe the idea of laying my scars bare in front of the gentle readers had to do something with His mercy.

Before I joined hands with serenity, my heart always felt the presence of a storm within it. The honking and distant sirens gave me a sense of annoyance whenever I walked across the city, as if they were screaming a story of distress. These loud, hollow voices reminded me of myself. Look at me closely; I was ready to prattle about my life, but was there a person willing to listen to my woes?

And if I talk about the noises haunting me, they could not drown out the hollowness within me. I could see my life falling apart, but I had no intention of keeping it intact. To tell you the truth, I never felt like living after my loved ones betrayed me for a man who did not share the family history with them. Do you question the source of this discord? It was none other than my blood family. The people who were meant to be my protector turned out to be my tormentors. But I was not entirely blameless—trusting too much in them caused me to be emotionally wrecked. Even my mother, who should have shielded me from this storm, turned a blind eye to my pain. I wonder how she remained unburdened by my remorse while she celebrated the happiness of a man who bruised her daughter for fifteen long years.

How should I tell the world my greatest weakness for my family was why I wanted to give up on life? I could not lie; there were times when I yearned for them to return to me. Believe me when I say I would have accepted them if they had whispered an apology in my ears lightly or maybe if they had given me a clue that they regretted betraying me. I could not track how many days turned into the night as I waited for them desperately, yet they never returned. My anguish was never about vengeance; there was no desire for blood, but I had the urge to reconcile. I wanted them to acknowledge the hurt they embossed within me and recognize the wreckage they had created. Nonetheless, it took me long enough to accept that my destruction was their win.

However, God did not let me smash to smithereens. He held me closely and did not let me go astray. Even during the worst phase of my life, when the rope that connected me to hope was almost broken, He ensured my safety and guided me toward the way that helped me find myself among the imposters.

Whenever I questioned myself—how can I move forward in life with this rotten wound as if nothing ever happened? My Lord crafted paths for me. Whenever I pondered over reconciling, He reminded me I did not need anyone to stand firm. And now, when I look at my past, and the years I poured into a relationship that ultimately left me shattered—physically, emotionally, and mentally, I thank God for not making me return to the people who prayed for my downfall. My sibling, my mother—the love that I tried holding onto for fifteen years, they all were never meant to be mine. They always had malicious thoughts; they wanted to inflict pain on my soul, yet God did not let me fall for their trap—He saved me from the bigger loss.

The truth was I might have to bear all the pain alone, but at least I was far away from any human danger. As their mask fell off, I made peace with my reality, and that was when God instilled a silver lining from the knowledge that I was not alone. Others may have relied on evilness, but I endured the gut-wrenching weight of abandonment and betrayal because God was with me. This hurt, though extremely agonizing, cut my delusion in half and shattered my self-made place for love, revealing the world in its raw form.

Suddenly, it dumped all the misery of the world on me but also opened my eyes to the hate people were brewing behind my back. They never reciprocated my love, and I always offered to fill their void with the pieces I had gathered for myself, neglecting the holes they were constantly perforating within me.

Day and night, I wept to receive their love, even when they collectively deceived me. I knew it was not normal to cry over the people who only wanted to destroy me, but the people in question were my family. As a human being, I naturally craved love and affection from the people I call family, but all they had was hate and maliciousness to offer in return. Their hearts were a blend of horror and dirth—I pity them and the person they have become.

Perhaps that was the reason why God distanced me from such evil energy. The more they tried to put a wicked spell on my life, the keen I became to activities that soothe the storm within me. I did not realize when life took me away from the roads of negativity and brought me a lot closer to the land of positivity. I was still struggling and fighting my battles, but I was no longer waiting for someone to come and conquer on my behalf. I was sure the road ahead of me would not be any smoother, but I did not fear a thing—I had God in my heart and was proud of the person I was becoming gradually.

Sometimes, my mind became a battlefield of memories where I desired to return to the good old days. I searched for the childhood where purity was our savior, but all that was left were fragments of our broken ties. The affection, I realized, had been my cruelest fantasy that would never come real. No matter how much I tried, I never seemed to receive the love I deserved. But when did resentment provide me with peace? I knew if I continued living with the hatred in my heart, I would become a prisoner of their thoughts, and this reality disgusted me.

Instead of holding them accountable for all the evilness, I focused on the path of forgiveness. It was a slow journey that required a great amount of patience, but here I was, fighting the anger that was telling me to slay all those who hurt me. But was I ready to let my healing go in vain? I might not be the most patient person on the earth, but as I took the path that reconnected me to Him, I realized no worldly thing could snatch my peace ever. I believed God gave me the unbearable pain so that I would not become one of them, and look at me: vengeance was no longer my desire. I did not crave the pain they inflicted on me; I desired never to fall prey to their evilness. Now, I was standing at the point where I had learned my trials were never my punishments but lessons—lessons in discernment, building walls wisely, and choosing companions who would cherish my existence and not daydream of poisoning my life by spewing some baseless lies.

I know the path I have decided to walk on; the path of spirituality will not be easy. There will be setbacks and moments when I feel injustice creeping inside my home. There will be times when the ghosts of the past will threaten me with their presence. But tonight, when I meticulously craft the final pages, I vow never to let my soul crumble. I make this pact to learn from the past without being consumed by it. I would not give up on myself; I would choose love and trust but with open eyes; it is a commitment to myself. The road ahead is long for sure, but for the first time in a long time, I want to fight to get myself back from despair. Yet, I cannot guarantee how long it will take. Maybe a year or two, but my fight to protect myself from demons will persist until I refuse to surrender.

I am proud of my journey, and even though I have come a long way, I have encountered times when I regressed to those haunting nights, especially whenever social media challenged my healing, reminding me about the betrayal I had received. Not long ago, I came across my ex-boyfriend, who was still hanging out with the girls he told me not to worry about. I remember how badly he shattered my trust in remaining friends with those women I had suspected. But he never cared about the dagger he placed in my heart; for him, our relationship was a mere joke. Yet, as painful as it was, I decided to walk away to protect my peace. It was a sane decision since my peace of mind was no longer hostage to his actions.

The only thing that still hurts me is my longing for my grandchild. I am still learning to live a life where I would not crave to have her single glimpse, but even if a day like this ever came, I assure myself I will never stop loving her. My daughter may have alienated her from me, but I will never forget her innocent smile. My burden is too heavy to bear alone, so I surrender to a higher power, forgetting all that could permit darkness into me. My aches needed to be placed in divine hands; that is the only place I could trust my vulnerability.

My God is the witness to my struggles, the keeper of my true heart. He would lead me to a new life where I would be cherished and empowered, not one that dragged me down. I have shed the old me behind, and as the metamorphosis of my soul continues, I will never fall back to my previous pattern. I have decided never to beg anyone to believe in me. The young version of me might have wanted to be believed when my mother accused me of stealing candy or maybe when my boyfriend assassinated my character, but remember, I am no longer the same person. My character does not need validation from those who cannot see its worth. God knows I never committed adultery or never stole the candy— He is my audience now, and for him alone would I strive.

Made in the USA
Columbia, SC
01 May 2025

416ea1ac-35d3-4bdd-819c-09ffcedd881eR01